**A PHENOMENOLOGICAL STUDY OF SELF-INITIATED
EXPATRIATE ADJUSTMENT**

A PHENOMENOLOGICAL STUDY OF SELF-INITIATED EXPATRIATE ADJUSTMENT

A dissertation submitted

by

DAVID DUSHAN NELSON

January, 2016

to

School of Organizational Leadership

UNIVERSITY OF THE ROCKIES

Upon the recommendation of the Faculty and the approval of the Board of Trustees, this dissertation is hereby accepted in partial fulfillment of the requirements for the degree of

DOCTOR OF PSYCHOLOGY

Approved by:

_____

Irene F. Stein, PhD
Committee Chair

Committee Members:
Jason M. Etchegaray, PhD
Marlon F. Sukal, PhD

1

A PHENOMENOLOGICAL STUDY OF SELF-INITIATED
EXPATRIATE ADJUSTMENT

A Phenomenological Study of Self-Initiated Expatriate Adjustment
By
David Dushan Nelson

Abstract

The focus of the present study was on exploring and examining the meaning and experience of sociocultural adjustment while being employed in the capacity of a self-initiated expatriate (SIE). The study sample consisted of 32 Western SIEs working in the Gulf Cooperation Council countries—Bahrain, Kuwait, Qatar, Saudi Arabia and United Arab Emirates—with a minimum of 2 years of successful contract completion in the education profession. Data were collected by conducting semistructured, in-depth interviews. The study data showed the SIEs defining of the experience as one or more of the following nine archetypes: the experience as more an epic of discovery than a career move, the experience as an adventure, a romantic quest, the chance to act as an explorer/world traveler, a boundaryless careerist, becoming an international citizen, an avenue of escape, the opportunity to act as the altruistic/hero, and fulfilling the role of a lifelong learner. Furthermore, the study results showed that motivation was critical in the sensemaking process and that as the SIE's definition of the experience as a successful endeavor may be rooted in the degree to which the SIE demonstrates a perception of growth in areas of communication, tolerance, patience, increased self-confidence, and fulfillment toward self-actualization. The data also indicated that personality plays a key factor in adjustment.

Key words: *self-initiated expatriate adjustment, sociocultural adjustment, expatriate experience, cultural shock, acculturation, cultural learning, coping and stress, identity, protean career, career success, career capital, global careers, globalization, performance, satisfaction, reasons to expatriate.*

A PHENOMENOLOGICAL STUDY OF SELF-INITIATED
EXPATRIATE ADJUSTMENT

ACKNOWLEDGMENTS

My thanks and appreciation to the members of my dissertation committee, Dr. Marlon Sukal and Dr. Jason Etchegaray, who generously gave their time and expertise to help me to better my work. I thank them for their contribution, their insights, and their support.

My thanks and appreciation to Dr. Irene Stein for persevering with me as my dissertation chair throughout the time it took me to complete this research and write the dissertation. Besides the normal administrative concerns that the position entails, she had to cope with the additional logistical entanglements that my geographical distance of 8,000 miles, time zone computations, and unbelievable time and resource challenges of my Middle East residency that were perhaps the most interesting and entertaining part of the journey. Throughout this entire process, from classroom to conception and execution, Dr. Stein was an excellent mentor and teacher.

DEDICATION

Throughout my life I have been blessed to be surrounded with strong supportive women. I would like to dedicate this thesis to my mother, Nancy, who had the greatest influence on who I am today and still watches me from above. To my beautiful daughter, Shandi, our time together watching you journey from child to wife and mother has been one of the most important and formative experiences of my life. And last but not least, my wife, Laurie. My muse, my inspiration. You encouraged me during those difficult and trying times by observing. Your presence, strength, faith, and patience kept me working when I wanted to give up. This dissertation would not have happened without your support.

A PHENOMENOLOGICAL STUDY OF SELF-INITIATED
EXPATRIATE ADJUSTMENT

TABLE OF CONTENTS

LIST OF TABLES

LIST OF FIGURES

LIST OF APPENDICES

CHAPTER I: INTRODUCTION

Globalization has led to a significant increase in the phenomenon of expatriation. As technologies and economies become more intertwined and competition increases, expatriate success has become more of a mitigating factor in the overall success of an organization competing in the international forum (Lee & Sukco, 2010). Changing economic conditions have made the phenomenon of expatriation a source of competitive opportunity for all stakeholders involved in the global labor markets (Howe-Walsh & Schyns, 2010). This new level of competition has led to changes in educational models for many countries that are emerging as developing world economic powers (Macionis & Plummer, 2008). One such region is the Middle East, specifically the oil-producing nations that comprise the Gulf Cooperation Council (GCC)—Bahrain, Kuwait, Oman, Qatar, Saudi Arabia, and the United Arab Emirates (UAE; Al Bawaba, 2012).

The phenomenon of expatriation is shifting from the traditional model of employees of an established home country organization sent to work in a satellite or subsidiary group of the

parent organization to a model of individuals who seek

employment on their own accord (Tharenou & Caulfield, 2010).

Education is one of the largest fields in which this shift is taking

place (Donnay, 2012). For the governments of these

economically and politically emerging GCC countries, the

globalization of education is seen as a competitive necessity

brought about by "the economic, political and societal forces

pushing 21st century higher education toward greater

international involvement" (Altbach & Knight, 2007, p. 290).

The question of what constitutes a successful expatriate

experience is far from having a consensus among researchers

(Yeo et al., 2011). Expatriates face the challenges of adjusting to

different cultures, languages, religions and social systems and

often come without organized systems to offer support (Brewster,

2002; Donnay, 2012; Tharenou & Caulfield, 2010; Yeo et al.,

2011). Expatriates often experience lack of emotional support,

grief, and feelings of isolation and loneliness, which may result in a crisis that manifests in early termination of the employment contract.

Much research has been conducted on the factors that contribute to *expatriate failure* and possible remedies to counteract these factors. Theories and models regarding the use of cross-cultural training, personality alignment, mentor programs, and increased compensation plans have been suggested as positive influences in adjustment, which is the influencer of success rates (Black, 1990; Crowley-Henry, 2007; Mendenhall & Oddou, 1985; Richardson, 2009; Shaffer, Harrison, Gregersen, Black, & Ferzandi, 2006; Tung, 1982, 1987). The focus of the present study was on exploring how self-initiated expatriates (SIEs) perceive and experience issues of adjustment, and particularly if and how adjustment to the living conditions of the GCC region was accomplished. Examining the adjustment of SIEs may present invaluable information to the organizations that recruit SIEs and to SIEs themselves.

Problem Background

The growing demand for talent to manage and grow businesses in global markets has led to an increase in the need and use of an expatriate workforce (Schuler & Tarique, 2007). The expatriate workforce is changing vastly from the traditional organizational expatriate (OE) sent abroad by a parent organization for a predetermined period of time to that of the emergence of the SIEs, individuals who search out and undertake employment outside of their home country without the support of or reliance on a home-country organization (Capellen & Janssens, 2005; Collings, Scullion, & Morley, 2007; Crowley-Henry, 2007; Inkson, Arthur, Pringle, & Barry, 1997). For the GCC nations—Bahrain, Kuwait, Oman, Qatar, Saudi Arabia, and the UAE—expatriates comprise 58% to 89% of the workforce with a predicted reliance on these levels through the year 2030 (Al Bawaba, 2012).

With the trend of growth primarily in the development of infrastructure and education sectors (International Labour Organization, 2013), SIEs will constitute a larger proportion of the international workforce in the GCC than OEs, mirroring

trends in the overall global market (International Labour

Organization, 2013; Tharenou & Caulfield, 2010). Current hiring

models, based on research conducted primarily using OEs, are

inadequate for efficiently and strategically staffing modern

organizations (Chen, 2012; Kealey, Protheroe, MacDonald, &

Vulpe, 2005). SIEs present a new paradigm in the Expat

workforce of which little is known (Chen, 2012; Kealey et al.,

2005).

Regions such as the GCC contain countries that

significantly rely on expatriate employees, estimated to be 58%

to 89% of the total workforce (Al Bawaba, 2012; Al-Waqfi,

2012). The need for organizations in the GCC region to

understand and develop strategies to effectively recruit and retain

SIEs is a critical factor for future success (Al-Waqfi, 2012;

Collings et al., 2007; Shin, Morgeson, & Campion, 2003).

Expatriate employee failure has significant financial

consequences for the overall economic status of these GCC

countries (Al Bawaba, 2012; Al-Rasheedi, 2012; Al-Waqfi,

2012). Replacing expatriate employees before their contract is completed can cost as much as $250,000 (Littrell, Salas, Hess, Paley, & Riedel, 2006). In addition to the outright financial costs, premature expatriate departure may create disengagement and subpar performance for the remaining staff (Klaff, 2002) and may negatively influence other valued employees, who may choose not to renew at the end of their contracts (Neill, 2008).

Expatriate failure has been defined as any termination of the employment relationship initiated by the organization or initiated by the expatriate employees themselves. Early terminations initiated by expatriate employees have been identified as a significant proportion of the known failed expatriate outcomes (Bozionelos, 2009). The GCC has been reported as experiencing expatriate turnover rates ranging from 32% to 90% (Al Bawaba, 2012; Al-Waqfi, 2012). Prior researchers have cited theories of culture shock as a predominate factor in expatriate failures (Black, 1990; Tung, 1982, 1987). Inability to adjust is attributed to the disconnect between the expatriate's values and beliefs and what the expatriate perceives as appropriate behavior in the new cultural environment (Black, 1990; Javidan, Dorfman, Sulley de Luque, & House, 2006; Maertz, Hassan, & Magnusson, 2009; Molinsky, 2007; Van Vianen, De Pater, Kristof-Brown, & Johnson, 2004).

Expatriate adjustment has been a topic of intense research and has developed as a major factor in the outcome of an expatriate assignment (Black, 1990; Black, Mendenhall, & Oddou, 1991; Mendenhall & Oddou, 1985; Shaffer & Harrison, 1998; Tung, 1981, 1982, 1984, 1987; Ward & Kennedy, 1992). Researchers have defined two distinct categories of expatriate adjustment (see Figure 1): psychological adjustment and sociocultural adjustment (Black, 1990; Black et al., 1991; Mendenhall & Oddou, 1985; Shaffer & Harrison, 1998; Ward & Kennedy, 1992). Psychological adjustment is defined as an overall sense of well-being, contentment, and happiness (Black, 1990; Shaffer & Harrison, 1998; Ward & Kennedy, 1992). Sociocultural adjustment has been broken into three facets that contribute to the expatriate's overall psychological comfort level: general adjustment, work adjustment, and interaction adjustment

(Black, 1990; Black et al., 1991; Mendenhall & Oddou, 1985;

Ward & Kennedy, 1992). General adjustment pertains to the

expatriate's psychological comfort level regarding the new host

culture's general living conditions and cultural practices. Work

adjustment describes the experienced comfort level regarding to

the new job responsibilities and the new work environment.

Interaction adjustment relates to the expatriate's comfort level

regarding communicating and interacting with members of the

host culture (Black et al., 1991; Mendenhall & Oddou, 1985;

Ward & Kennedy, 1992).

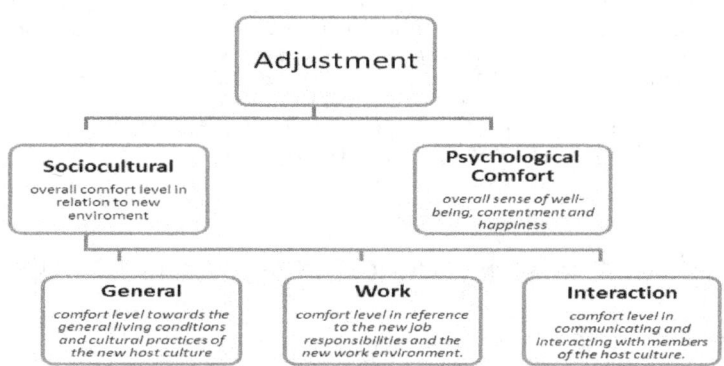

Figure 1. Expat adjustment theory. Based on concepts from "Toward a Comprehensive
Model of International Adjustment: An Integration of Multiple Theoretical Perspectives,"
by J. S. Black, M. Mendenhall, and G. Oddou, 1991. The Academy of Management Review,
16, 291–317. Copyright 1991 by the Academy of Management; "The Dimensions of
Expatriate Acculturation," by M. E. Mendenhall and G. Oddou, 1985. *Academy of
Management Review, 10*, 39–47. Copyright 1985 by the Academy of Management; and
"Locus of Control, Mood Disturbance and Social Difficulty During Cross-Cultural
Transitions," by C. Ward and A. Kennedy, 1992. *International Journal of Intercultural
Relations, 16*, 175–194. Copyright 1992 by Elsevier.

Haslberger and Brewster (2007) proposed a more detailed set of six adjustment domains based on the work of Navas et al. (2005, 2007). Haslberger and Brewster suggested that these six domains give a truer and more accurate depicture of the elements of adjustment for expatriates (see Figure 2).

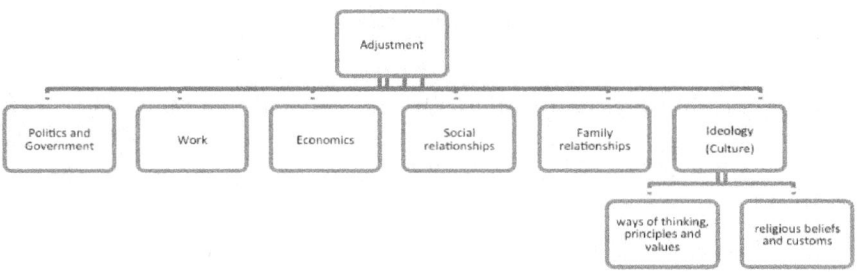

Figure 2. Expat adjustment elements. Based on concepts from "Relative Acculturation Model (RAEM): New Contributions With Regard to the Study of Acculturation," by M. Navas, M. C. Garcia, J. Sanchez, A. J. Rojas, P. Pumares, and J. S. Fernandez, 2005. *International Journal of Intercultural Relations, 29*, 21–37. Copyright 2005 by Elsevier; and "Acculturation Strategies and Attitudes According to the Relative Acculturation Extended Model (RAEM): The Perspectives of Natives Versus Immigrants," by M. Navas, M. C. Garcia, A. J. Rojas, P. Pumares, and J. S. Fernandez, 2007. *International Journal of Intercultural Relations, 31*, 67–86. Copyright 2007 by Elsevier.

Both theories as complementary theories of expatriate adjustment were used in the present study.

Study results have shown that SIEs, compared to OEs, show a higher level of general adjustment and interaction adjustment with host-country nationals yet maintain the same or higher turnover rates (Biemann & Andresen, 2010; Forseth-

Whitman & Isakovic, 2012; Peltokorpi & Froese, 2011).

Traditional factors of influence on expatriate failure rates may

not apply to SIEs (Fitzgerald & Howe-Walsh, 2008). Current

research on SIEs, which is predominantly empirical in nature, has

sparsely addressed issues of retention and expatriate success.

Elements such as motivation, repatriation planning, gender

difference, and resiliency have been mentioned as factors in SIE

success (Bartlett, Ghoshal, & Beamish, 2007; Capellen &

Janssens, 2005; Collings et al., 2007) but data on the extent of

influence on adjustment and success are scarce.

There is little known about why SIEs seek out and accept

expatriate assignments (Kealey et al., 2005). Research results

regarding OEs suggest that career development is the major

motivating factor for that group while desiring to initiate a

lifestyle and location change may be more influential factors for

SIEs undertaking self-initiated expatriation and working in an

international context (Fitzgerald & Howe-Walsh, 2008). Other

researchers have cited the need to examine the individual issues

SIEs face regarding how they establish relationships with their new organizations and how they adapt to new environments with no home organization for support (Mayerhofer, Hartmann, Michelitsch-Riedl, & Kollinger, 2004).

Problem Statement

SIEs constitute a larger proportion of the international workforce than traditional OEs (Crowley-Henry, 2007; Inkson et al., 1997; Tharenou & Caulfield, 2010). Global hiring trends indicate an increasing need of organizations to fill positions with SIEs, especially in the GCC region where expatriate employees comprise 90% of the total workforce in some countries (Al-Waqfi, 2012; Manpower (2010). Organizational ability to effectively recruit and retain SIEs is a critical factor for future success (Shin et al., 2003). The general problem is that current recruitment and retention models are based on research specific to OEs and are inadequate for predicting levels of adjustment and retention success among SIEs (Chen, 2012). To better manage and understand SIEs, organizations need information on effective strategies and methodologies for retaining the employees they hire (Al-Waqfi, 2012; Arthur, Khapova, & Wilderon, 2005; Collings et al., 2007; Shin et al., 2003; Yan, Zhu, & Douglas, 2002).

Adjustment has been identified as a major component of expatriate retention and success (Javidan et al., 2006; Maertz et al., 2009; Molinsky, 2007; Van Vianen et al., 2004). Adjustment is composed of two constructs: (a) psychological, and (b) sociocultural, with the subsets of general adjustment, work adjustment, and interaction adjustment with host-country nationals (Bhaskar-Shrinivas, Shaffer, & Luk, 2005; Black, 1990; Searle & Ward, 1990). The specific problem is that adjustment can be a major negative factor in an expatriate's contract completion or success. Results from further research have indicated that SIEs when compared to OEs show a higher level of general environment/culture adjustment and interaction adjustment with host-country nationals yet maintain the same and in many cases higher turnover rates than their OE counterparts (Biemann & Andresen, 2010; Forseth-Whitman & Isakovic, 2012; Peltokorpi & Froese, 2009). The high turnover rate has a significant negative impact on the GCC region's organizational competitiveness and overall economic condition (Manpower, 2010).

Purpose of the Study

The purpose of this qualitative, interpretative phenomenological study was to explore the meaning and experience of sociocultural adjustment while being employed as an SIE. The research sample consisted of 32 SIEs who worked in the countries of Bahrain, Kuwait, Oman, Qatar, Saudi Arabia, and the UAE at the time of the study. Participants were from Western countries (Australia, Canada, Great Britain, Ireland, New Zealand, South Africa and the United States) with a minimum of 2 years of successful contract completion in the education profession who were employed by host organizations in the aforementioned Arab nations. Data were gathered through semistructured in-depth interviews. This allowed the participants to describe the experience and identify elements they perceived, express feelings associated with those elements, and identify perceptions of stressors/motivators experienced during their adjustment process. Semistructured in-depth interviews were deemed most appropriate to describe the SIEs' perceived meanings within the contexts of the expatriate experience (Giorgi, 2008; Hegel, 1977; Heidegger, 1962; Husserl, 1970; van Manen, 1990; Wertz, 2005) and how the SIEs defined a successful or failed experience.

Qualitative interpretative phenomenological analysis (IPA) research was an appropriate application to gain an understanding of "the perspective of the person or persons being studied" (Willis, 2007, p. 107) through the detailed description of those who concretely lived the phenomenon (Giorgi, 2008; Hegel, 1977; Heidegger, 1962; Husserl, 1970; van Manen, 1990; Wertz, 2005). IPA allows for an inductive methodology to explore the participants' perceptions and lived experiences while allowing the researcher to gain insight on how the participants make sense of their experience (Smith, 2004, 2007).

Understanding the essence of the phenomenon is derived through the development of different perspectives through dialogue and then by charting any similarities or commonalities among the participants' perspectives (Smith, 2004, 2007). By allowing those who have experienced the phenomenon of sociocultural adjustment experienced by SIE to describe the perceptions of the what, how, and why in the context of their situations, a greater understanding of the experience may assist those currently participating in or contemplating SIE.

Importance of the Study

By concentrating on the SIE experience, this study is of significance for the GCC countries with a critical reliance on expatriate labor, some as high as 90% of the total workforce (Al-Waqfi, 2012). Expatriate failure such as early termination of the contract, disengagement, and subpar performance translates into substantial organizational costs for GCC countries. Most research efforts to date have focused on traditional OEs sent by a parent organization for predetermined period of time with organization support and a predetermined repatriation plan. There are very limited data concerning the uniqueness and differences of the SIE phenomenon.

The current trend in the global expatriate workforce

marketplace shows a significant shift from the traditional OE to

SIE (Alsehan, Forstenlechner, & Al-Nakeeb, 2010; Tharenou &

Caulfield, 2010). The emergence of SIEs, individuals who search

out and undertake employment outside of their home country, has

not been studied in detail (Capellen & Janssens, 2005; Collings et

al., 2007; Crowley-Henry, 2007; Inkson et al., 1997). There are

many questions related to the SIE experience whose answers are

crucial for organizations wishing to strategically staff for success

and avoid the high financial impact of expatriate employment

failure (Alsehan et al. 2010; Al-Waqfi, 2012; Chen, 2012;

Tharenou & Caulfield, 2010). Results from earlier research

indicated differences between OEs and SIEs regarding variables

of motivation for acceptance of employment, compensation, and

repatriation goals (Inkson et al., 1997; Suutari & Brewster, 2000),

but further research is needed to explore the concepts of

subjective well-being, adjustment, and success as applied to SIEs

(Biemann & Andresen, 2010; Chen, 2012; Peltokorpi & Froese,

2009; Tharenou & Caulfield, 2010). It was hoped that this study would provide insights on how successful SIEs have experienced adjustment, which could allow avenues for current and potential SIEs to plan and develop practical support systems that allow for success and personal growth through the SIE experience.

Study Design

Because of a shortage of literature about the SIE experience, an exploratory approach was considered most appropriate for the present study (Dickmann & Harris, 2005; Richardson, 2006). The present study was qualitative rather than quantitative. Qualitative methodology does not assume there is a single or objective reality to be uncovered but instead guides data collection and analysis techniques by clustering raw data into sub- and superordinate themes to build a detailed picture of the phenomenon in question (Smith, 2004, 2007). Data for the present study were collected by conducting semistructured in-depth interviews. IPA was used to engage with individuals' sensemaking of lived experiences. Qualitative IPA is an appropriate application to gain an understanding of "the perspective of the person or persons being studied" (Willis, 2007,

p. 107) through the detailed description of those who concretely

lived the phenomenon (Smith, 2004, 2007; Smith, Flowers, &

Osborn, 1997).

The sample consisted of 32 SIE participants who were

currently working in the GCC countries—Bahrain, Kuwait,

Oman, Qatar, Saudi Arabia and the UAE. Participants were from

Western countries (Australia, Canada, Great Britain, Ireland,

New Zealand, South Africa and the United States) with a

minimum of 2 years of successful contract completion in the

education profession and who were employed by host

organizations in the aforementioned Arab nations at the time of

the study. Through purposive sampling, data gathered from the

semistructured interviews allowed searching for any common

experiences as well as understanding consist of the assigned

meanings of any given unique experience from the individual

participant's perspective. The coding of specific elements of the

shared experience (phenomenon) allowed for interpretation,

which provided information to add to the current body of

knowledge (Smith, 2004, 2007). IPA enables an open-ended

dialogue between researchers and participants, allowing

researchers to reflect on their own preconceptions. I accounted

for my own preconceptions and attitudes, set them aside,

evaluated the statements and observations of the study

participants, and determined how the experiences of the study

participants and the meaning the participants have applied to

those experiences may be applied to existing theories (Smith,

2004, 2007). By allowing those who have experienced the

phenomenon of SIE to describe the perceptions of the what, how,

and why in the context of their situations, a greater understanding

of the experience may be developed that could assist future

strategic planning for both potential employers and SIEs.

Research Questions

The following research question was the central focus of

the present study: What is the lived experience and meaning

attached to the experience of sociocultural adjustment of a native

Western SIE while employed in the Near East? Responses to this

research question also informed two related questions: How do

SIEs employed in the Near East experience sociocultural

adjustment in terms of their work, their interaction with members of the host culture, and in adjusting to the general living conditions and cultural practices of the new host culture; and how do SIEs employed in the Near East attach meaning to their sociocultural adjustment?

Theoretical Framework

According to Moustakas (1994), phenomenological research is employed to examine the base of knowledge derived from beliefs and perceptions of those who have experienced the phenomenon. Phenomenological research looks at the essence of the experience to gain an understanding of the individual's "perceptions, perspectives, and understandings of an event that occurred in their lives" (Leedy & Ormrod, 2010, p. 144). The theoretical foundation for the purpose of this research study was an exploration of the lived experience of the SIE as it relates to adjustment and success. The following theoretical models formed the foundation in determining that understanding.

Culture

Culture is the foundation of shared values and beliefs that form the dimensions of a group's unification and identity and influence the development of social structure, behavior, ethics, and cognitive frameworks for the group and individual (Hofstede, 1998; House, Hanges, Mansour, Dorfman, & Gupta, 2004; Mallehi, 2007; Morgan, 1986; Pothukuchi, Damanpour, Choi, Chen, & Park, 2002; Schein, 2004; Tayeb, 2005; Trompenaars & Hamden-Turner, 2000). Based on Hofstede's (1980) study, culture has four dimensions—power distance, uncertainty avoidance, individualism versus collectivism, and masculinity versus femininity. While societies are not completely homogeneous, they tend to develop patterns and preferences that allow for classifying them as individualistic or collectivistic in general (Hofstede, 1980).

Within a culture there may be subcultures and divisions known as ingroups and outgroups (C. W. L. Hill, 2003; Schein, 1995; Tayeb, 1988). The shared foundations of history, religion, language, education, and economic and political philosophy influence individuals to behave and share

similar attitudes and perceptions (C. W. L. Hill, 2003;

Hofstede, 2001). Hofstede's model of cultural dimensions is

one the most recognized and accepted model of cultural

dimensions (Adler, 2007; Askary, Pounder, & Yazdifar,

2008; Bass, 1990; Fougere & Moulettes, 2006; Oshlyansky,

Cairns, & Thimbleby, 2006; Triandis, 2004).

Hofstede (1980) determined a model that

distinguishes the values of individual cultures and the

influence these values have in the workplace. The original

model consisted of four clusters: individualism versus

collectivism, power distance, masculinity versus femininity,

and uncertainty avoidance. Numerical values associated with

each dimension are used in a comparison model to

acknowledge differences. Hofstede added a fifth dimension

measuring time orientation based on 1991 research he

conducted with Bond. A sixth dimension measuring

indulgence versus restraint was also added based on the

research of Minkov and Hofstede (2011). Hofstede

emphasizes that the measurement scores are relative and based on comparison to other cultures, making scores without comparison meaningless

Culture Shock

Oberg (1960) is credited with the term *culture shock*, which he defined as "occupational disease of people who have been suddenly transplanted abroad [and is] precipitated by the anxiety that results from losing all our familiar signs and symbols of social intercourse" (p. 177). Several researchers have examined the cycle of culture shock and attributed the expatriate's lack of understanding and inability to cope with the stresses from environmental changes they were experiencing as a source of failure in assignment completion (Black, 1990; Black & Mendenhall, 1990; Mendenhall & Oddou, 1985; Tung, 1982, 1987). The process of culture shock consists of four stages, which are commonly referred to as the U-curve theory of adjustment (Gullahorn & Gullahorn, 1963).

Sensemaking Theory

Sensemaking is a theory that explains the process by which an individual determines understanding and gives relevance to an experience. The process involves behaviors, communication, and cognition and the assessment of value and meaning for the individual (Cavaleri & Reed, 2008; Cheuk, 2008; Dervin, 1998). The meanings are extremely individually oriented and may often be incomplete or blocked (Olsson, 2009; Weick & Sutcliffe, 2005), which in turn can cause the individual to seek out information both formally and informally to complete the sensemaking process.

Decision Theory

Decision theory is used to predict and explain choices and to improve the decision-making process (Peterson, 2009). Complex decisions most often present an individual with a difficult dilemma; high levels of uncertainty add to this dilemma (Fischer, Fischer, Weisweiler, & Frey, 2010). The difference between a good decision and a bad decision is often determined by the balance of influence of the individual's needs and intuition and a careful analysis of the positive and negative consequences

of the decision alternatives (Fischer et al., 2010).

Psychological Adjustment

The feeling of well-being, happiness, and contentment are

the components of psychological adjustment (Black, 1990;

Shaffer & Harrison 1998; Ward & Kennedy, 1992). Researchers

have defined three types of adjustment: general living,

interaction, and work (Black, 1990; Black & Stephens, 1989;

Gregerson & Black, 1990; Huang, Chi & Lawler, 2005;

Nicholson, 1984; Oberg, 1960). The division of two components

of psychological adjustment into the areas of sociocultural

adjustment and general adjustment (Black, 1990; Black et al.,

1991; Mendenhall & Oddou, 1985; Ward & Kennedy, 1992) was

applied in this study.

SIEs

Little is truly known about SIEs as the established body of

research has been developed by studying the traditional OE and

has relied heavily on the perspectives and definitions of

adjustment derived from organizations (Biemann & Andresen,

2010; Bonache, Brewster, & Suutari, 2007; Bruggeman, 2010).

As the growing population of SIEs becomes more important in

the international business community, and specifically the GCC,

there is a need for greater understanding of the phenomenon of

the SIE, the elements that constitute the phenomenon, the factors

that influence the phenomenon, and the models and applications

that can be developed and applied for the successful recruitment,

retention, and outcomes desired by the organizations that employ

SIEs as well as the SIEs themselves. A reasonable assumption is

that SIEs can contribute to the general data pool through the

transfer of knowledge in accurately representing and defining the

experience, leading to a greater understanding of the SIE

phenomenon (Ratcliff, 2007). The current study was formulated

to help develop a greater understanding of the process of SIE

adjustment as well as the meanings of SIE adaptation, the

definition of success as perceived by SIE, and clarification as to

whether any contrast may be found with that of the well-

documented OE experience, leading to a deeper understanding of

the SIE phenomenon.

Definition of Terms

The meaning of a word or a series of words, terms, or phrases is critical for a clear and concise understanding of meaning in a research study. The following terms and definitions were employed in the current research study:

Adjustment: the process of altering or adapting behavior to reach an acceptance or a balanced relationship with a new environment (Black, 1988; Black et al., 1991; Mendenhall & Oddou, 1985; Shaffer & Harrison 1998; Ward & Kennedy, 1992).

Expatriate: temporary employees of business and/or government organizations who are not native residents of the host country or culture where the business and/or government organization operates. The time period is generally of duration between 6 months and 5 years (Aycan & Kanungo, 1997).

OE: employees assigned by their current organization to perform their current or related job functions abroad in one the organizations subsidiaries (Inkson et. al, 1997). *Perception*: The use of sensory information to attain Expatriate awareness and understanding of an environment (Foust-Cummings,

Sabattini, & Carter 2008).

SIEs: individuals who decide independently of an

organization to migrate to another country in search of work

(Brewster & Suutari, 2005; Inkson, 1997; Mol, Born, Willemsen,

Nijmegen, & Van der Molen, 2005).

Sensemaking: the cognitive appraisal of a specific event

and the related emotions and responses generated that result in an

individual's choice of action (Klein, 1998).

Limitations

Snape and Spencer (2003) stated the importance of

recognizing the potential pitfalls and weakness of any study to be

undertaken. The current phenomenological research study had

the following limitations. The first limitation was the small

sample size and unique homogony of the study. It was not

presumed that this study would represent all SIEs. There are

several unique groups of SIEs, and their experiences may differ

vastly due to different factors among these groups. Care was taken to avoid wide generalizations when discussing the experiences of the participants in the present study.

Second, while the region in which this study's sample was gathered may share common values in its cultural influences and the influence of its Islamic tradition, each GCC country maintains a unique niche. While collectivist in nature, the clan and tribe structure of the region and the uniqueness each country brings to its social order may have a limiting influence on the generalizability of any reported experiences.

Third, the GCC region is in a position of economic prosperity that provides a relatively low cost of living while offering relatively high expatriate salaries that afford the opportunity for a higher standard of living compared to other regions of the world. This economic anomaly may have had a skewing effect on the experiences of this study's participants. As previously stated, care was taken to avoid the assumption that there was a single and objective reality to be uncovered.

Fourth, there was a dependence on the participants' willingness and ability to accurately and honestly share their perceptions and experiences during the interview process. I paid

special attention to building trust and ensuring strict controls for

confidentiality to help encourage participation. Additionally,

participants were guided through the semistructured interview

process by the interviewer asking predetermined key questions

designed to elicit responses within the study's boundaries and

direction in order to acquire the desired data.

The last limitation was my own potential bias, as I am an

SIE. As such, I paid attention to setting aside my bias and

personal experiences (Creswell, 2005; Leedy & Ormrod, 2010) as

not to influence what I heard participants saying. Using *epoché*,

or bracketing, during the interview process and transcription of

responses helped mitigate bias (B. Baker, 2006; Creswell, 2009;

Giorgi, 2008; Moustakas, 1994; Neuman, 2006; Polkinghorne,

2005; Smith 2004, 2007).

Delimitations

Delimitations allow for a study to be limited and help

define that which is not included or intended in the study (B.

Baker, 2006; Creswell, 2009; Giorgi, 2008; Leedy & Ormrod,

2010; Moustakas, 1994; Neuman, 2006). It was acknowledged that the qualitative design and small sample size may limit the present study's generalization. The small sample size also gave rise to concerns regarding the ability to achieve saturation as well as potential limits to the type and amount of data received (Marshall & Rossman, 2006; Patton, 2002). It was also acknowledged that the focused geographic region of the study may likely not represent experiences of SIEs in other geographic regions. Still, the study was specific to the experiences of this particular sample and might "have applicability in other contexts" (D. J. Cohen & Crabtree, 2006, para. 1), thus requiring strict attention in maintaining a detailed description of the methodology and findings.

The decision to include participants based on the criterion of a minimum of 2 years experience also presented a limitation on the sample size. It was not possible to state conclusions about individual stratum such as gender, marital status, age, and professional background.

Assumptions

It was recognized that the self-report nature of the present study's design may have resulted in the subjects providing what they deemed as socially desirable data, which may have led to compromising the reliability and accuracy of the data recorded. I was confident that the measures of maintaining participant confidentiality and anonymity would belay any fears of undesirable social outcomes for participants. I was also confident in the research-based generalization of educators as individuals with a high social consciousness that leads to strong, defined moral values regarding helping and serving others as part of their social responsibility (Drliková, 1992; Kačáni, 2004; Zelina, 1996).

Summary

This introductory chapter includes an outline of the area of study, a delineation of the problem and background of the phenomenon under study, and an overview of the research purpose, context, and methodology. This phenomenological study posited the potential for increasing the understanding of the

SIE's experience of sociocultural adjustment through an examination of the perceptions of the lived experience as defined by the SIE. Study results may provide a better focus on issues contributing to failure of accomplishing assignment goals and allow for developing strategies that promote and increase the probability of success for the SIE and the organizations that rely on these individuals. Chapter II provides the theoretical background and foundation for the present study through the examination of the relevant literature.

CHAPTER II: LITERATURE REVIEW

The purpose of this literature review was to examine existing research regarding the expatriate phenomenon, identify existing gaps in the research, and to establish a theoretical foundation for the present study. The literature review included academic research that provided the explanation and theories needed for understanding the background, development, and current direction of research concerning the expatriate phenomenon as well as the emergence of the SIE phenomenon. Chapter II contains an in-depth discussion of elements of the expatriate phenomenon through the examination of peer-reviewed articles, books, documents, and dissertations. Databases used for the literature review included ProQuest and EBSCOhost, which were accessed through the University of the Rockies Electronic Library System. In addition, Sheikh Zayed University, Birkbeck College University of London, and the Emirates Center for Strategic Studies and Research databases were also extensively accessed. Internet resources included SAGE Full-Text Collections and Google Scholar. Several government databases also yielded studies and statistical information that added support to the study's purpose and foundation. The topics searched reinforced the existing gap in data related to the study problem.

Overview

Chapter I introduced the topic of expatriation and defined the distinction of the two expatriate categories: OEs and SIEs. Also presented was a rationale for the significance of research on the phenomenon of the lived experience of the SIEs being immersed into a foreign culture, that their perspectives concerning the issues, challenges, and adjustments that effect success may provide a better understanding of the phenomenon. The purpose of Chapter II was to develop a synthesis of the extant literature; that is, what is currently understood concerning the phenomenon, and to provide justification for the present study. Because of the vastness of the topic of expatriation, I chose to establish a framework for presenting the extant literature by identifying key components of the phenomenon from the literature. The framework consists of an introduction to expatriation, the role of culture, the differences in individualistic versus collectivistic society, and the influence the norms and rules of each of the aforementioned area's exhibit in the SIE process of adjustment, sensemaking, expatriate management, and the growth of the phenomenon in the GCC. These theories and concepts are all critical factors in an individual's ability to experience the feelings of belonging, self-identity, and fitting in (Goffman, 1966; E. T. Hall, 1992; M. R. Hall & Hall, 1975).

This study's central focus was the adjustment experiences of Western SIEs, who come from predominately individualistic cultures, as they experienced living in a Near Eastern collectivist society. Creswell (2003) discussed the social, cultural, and material influences of intrapsychic connections between individuals and their surroundings. How SIEs process their experiences and the value and meaning they assign to these experiences is considered influential in the SIE adjustment experience.

Chapter II provides an overview of the research regarding the phenomenon of expatriation, the emergence of SIEs, and current theories of expatriate adjustment. The models of culture, culture shock, and their roles in expatriate adjustment are also examined.

Introduction to Expatriation

The purpose of the following section is to introduce the concept of expatriation. The topics discussed are the historical perspective of expatriation, the definition of an expatriate, the differentiation between OEs and SIEs, and research findings on expatriation.

History of Expatriation

Expatriation is not a new phenomenon. It has existed for centuries, but in the modern era it has become a substantial component of the global economy (Richards, 1996; Stenning, 1994; Suzuki, 1998). The 1950s saw the emergence of large international charitable organizations that provided education, religious evangelism, disaster relief, and socioeconomic development for various countries throughout Asia and Africa (Suzuki, 1998). The next two decades experienced an expansion of international trade with the introduction of new trade legislation in the United States (Richards, 1996). As financial

and human capital investment grew for organizations, research

began on how individuals responded to new circumstances of

employment (Gullahorn & Gullahorn, 1963) and cultural change

(Oberg, 1954, 1960). As organizations began expanding abroad

and employees were moved from within the organization to head

foreign offices the focus became that of individual characteristics

that contributed to efficiency and assignment success (G. M.

Guthrie & Zektick, 1967).

The 1970s saw Japanese success in establishing

international offices and highlighted a focus on the transferability

of systems and cross-cultural issues as they related to individuals

assigned to operate within the systems (J. C. Baker & Ivancevich,

1971; Brislin, 1981; Brislin, Lommer, & Thorndike, 1973; Tung,

1981). The next two decades saw a shift in the research focus

toward training and preparation of expatriate employees.

Research was conducted to determine what types and methods of

training and preparation would be the most effective and would

prove most efficient with the smallest cost to the organization

(Adler, 1981; J. C. Baker & Ivancevich, 1971; Black &
Mendenhall, 1989; Black et al., 1991; Naumann, 1993; Triandis,
Malpass, & Davidson, 1973; Tung, 1981). It was also during this
period that elements of repatriation and organizational
commitment related to employee mobility and commitment came
under study (Adler, 1981; Black, Gregersen, & Mendenhall,
1992; Luthans, McCaul, & Dodd, 1985). Retention and success
of expatriate employees were also examined for specific factors
of influence critical to successful assignment completion. Role
importance and impact of diversity, resiliency, flexibility, gender,
family, and organizational environment became the focus of
study (Adler, 1984; Bartlett & Ghoshal, 1989; Black &
Gregersen, 1991; Briody & Chrisman, 1991; Coyle, 1986;
Harvey, 1985).

The emergence of women in the expatriate workforce
began in the 1990s (H. Harris, 1995, 1999; Linehan & Walsh,
2000). This new workforce demographic required examining
what influences were developing in expatriate retention and how
human resource departments could articulate successful

recruitment and maintain a higher rate of retention with possible

foresight toward factors that increase retention during the

selection of expatriate employees (Black et al., 1991; Brett, Stoh,

& Reilly, 1992; Forster, 1994; Suutari & Brewster, 1998).

Researchers began examining the developing trend of dual-career

expatriates and what potential influences and effects the trend

would have concerning the expatriate phenomenon (Glanz & van

der Sluis, 2001; Harvey, Buckley, Novicevic, & Wiese 1999;

Peiperl & van der Sluis, 1999; C. R. Smith, 1994). Other

researchers began examining the role of interaction and

relationship between the host nationals and the expatriate

employee and the value of cross-cultural training (Hailey 1996;

Mayerhofer, Hartmann, & Herbert, 2004; Mayerhofer et al.,

2004; Perkins & Hendry, 1999; Sparrow, 1999). The latter half

of the 1990s brought a focus on compensation packages,

relocation policies, organizational costs, critical skills needed,

and management theory regarding the length of stay and type of

expatriate assignment (Brewster, Harris, & Petrovic, 2001;

Brewster & Scullion, 1997; Doz & Prahalad, 1986; Forster,

2000b; Tayeb, 1994).

Since 2000, the global market has seen an increase in the

use of an expatriate workforce (Bakker, 2009; Batt & Colvin,

2011; Boney, 2009; Caligiuri & Tarique, 2009; Mol et al., 2005;

Thorn, 2008). The start of the 21st century also saw a change in

the expatriate demographics with more positions being filled by

those who were not placed by a parent organization, and this

trend is expected to continue (Alsehan et al., 2010; Al-Waqfi,

2012; Biemann & Andresen, 2010; Chen, 2012; Tharenou &

Caulfield, 2010).

The emergence of the SIE (Inkson et al., 1997; Suutari &

Brewster, 2000) and the increasing growth in the global economy

has created the need for research. SIEs are considered to be the

largest segment of the expatriate population (Tharenou &

Caulfield, 2010), and there is a significant gap in the research on

SIE characteristics, how they fit into established retention and

recruitment models, and if there are enough data to adequately

predict the successful completion of expatriate assignments

(Biemann & Andresen, 2010; Chen, 2012; Peltokorpi & Froese,

2009; Tharenou & Caulfield, 2010). It has been argued that

retention and motivation models, based on OE workplace

behaviors, are inadequate for predicting the successful

completion of expatriate assignments (Chen, 2012; Mol et al.,

2005).

Definition of Expatriation

There is no consensus on the definition of expatriate.

Duckett (1999) provided a typical definition:

> Expatriate assignment is a job transfer that takes the
> employee to a work place that is outside the country in
> which he or she is a citizen . . . expatriate assignments are
> longer in duration than other types of international
> assignments and require the employee to move his or her
> entire household to the foreign location. (p. 101)

This definition is most often applied to individuals who

are sent by a parent organization for a predetermined time period

to work in the subsidiaries of multinational enterprises (Caligiuri,

Tarique, & Jacobs, 2009; E. Cohen, 1977; Dowling & Welch,

2004; Mayerhofer et al., 2004; Suutari & Brewster, 2000).

Woods (2003) expanded the definition by stating that expatriates

play a pivotal role to the organization's success and

competitiveness. The definition used in the present study was

Aycan and Kanungo's (1997), which states that expatriates are

> employees of business and government organizations who
> are sent by their organization to a related unit in a country
> which is different from their own, to accomplish a job or
> organization-related goal for a pre-designated temporary
> time period of usually more than six months and less than
> five years in one term. (p. 250)

Differentiators Between OEs and SIEs

The majority of existing literature dealing with

expatriation has been focusing mainly on the individual working

abroad in the subsidiaries of multinational enterprises (Al-Ariss,

2010; Inkson et al., 1997; Richardson & McKenna, 2003; Selmer

& Lauring, 2010; M. P. Smith, 2005; Suutari & Brewster, 2000;

Tharenou and Caulfield, 2010). These traditional OEs sent by

their parent companies are technically skilled and know the

organization's strategies, culture, and systems; are motivated by

career aspirations; and retain the goal of advancing in the same

organization when they return home (Caligiuri, 2000a; Caligiuri,

2000b; Connelly, Hitt, DeNisi, & Ireland, 2007; J. P. Guthrie,

Ash & Stevens, 2003; Holopainen & Björkman, 2005; Kanter,

1993; Linehan & Scullion, 2001; Selmer, 2001; Selmer & Leung,

2002). Cartus Research (2012) reported the following

demographics for OEs: 76% male, 71% ages 30 to 49 years, 69%

married.

Inkson et al. (1997) introduced the concept of SIEs,

individuals who take the initiative to relocate to a country for

career purposes, and several researchers who have studied the

phenomenon have found that SIEs differ significantly from OEs

in several demographic factors including experience, skillsets,

age, gender, and marital status (Al-Ariss, 2010; Banai & Harry,

2004; Bozionelos, 2009; Hipsher, 2008; Peltokorpi and Froese,

2009; Richardson, 2006, 2009; Richardson & McKenna, 2002;

Selmer & Lauring, 2010; Suutari & Brewster, 2000; Tharenou &

Caulfield, 2010; Vance, 2005). It has also been hypothesized that

motivation, level of organizational support, personality traits,

stress tolerance, and coping strategies differences between OEs

and SIEs may promote a higher level of challenges and that the

uncertainties regarding psychological security and comfort that

SIEs face are greater (Bozionelos, 2009; Capellen & Janssens,

2005; Collings et al., 2007; Crowley-Henry, 2007; Peltokorpi &

Froese, 2009; Richardson; 2009; Suutari & Brewster, 2000;

Tharenou & Caulfield, 2010). Other researchers have found that

SIEs are more adept at adjusting and less organizationally

dependent than OEs (Banai & Harry, 2004; Bozionelos, 2009;

Collings et al., 2007; Kohonen, 2005; Peltokorpi & Froese,

2009).

Culture as a Factor

Culture is a complex concept that has many definitions,

and no consensus on a single definition is found in the literature.

Hofstede (1980) defined culture as "the collective programming

of the mind which distinguishes the members of one group from

another" (p. 21). D. Hall (1976) discussed the nature of culture

as normative patterns of behavior that permeates throughout the

values and attitudes of a society. D. Hall further stated that while

culture is not genetically inherited it is shared and passed from

generation to generation, it is not static, and it can change over

periods of time. Kale (1996) and Mulholland (1991) discussed

the power of culture as an influence on an individual, being the first way people perceive values and beliefs, which in turn

provide the individual's orientation toward group and national

behavior. Culture influences nearly every aspect of an

individual's sense of identity and influences perception and

judgment in most settings and situations (Hofstede, 1980; Kale,

1996; Mulholland, 1991). Research has supported the notion that

a shared set of values and collective beliefs helps establish a

cognitive framework that influences behavioral norms, rituals,

and ethical codes, which in turn influences the shared meanings

and perceptions leading to people of the same national culture

behaving in a similar manner (Alvesson, 2002; Brown, 1995;

Hofstede, 1980; Kale, 1996; Kreitner & Kinicki, 1998; Morgan,

1986; Mulholland, 1991).

The Role of National Culture

Hofstede (2001) has stated the significant impact of

national culture concerning organizations and social structures.

National culture has been shown to influence methods of

leadership and management (Allen & Meyer, 1990; Hofstede,

1998, 2001; House et al., 2004; Mallehi, 2007; Pothukuchi et al.,

2002; Schein, 2004; Tayeb, 2005; Trompenaars & Hamden-Turner, 2000). An individual's commitment has been noted as a crucial aspect of success for any organization or project of social change (Coopey & Hartley, 1991; Hofstede, 2001; Meyer & Allen, 1990; Swales, 2000). While several researchers have examined the importance of commitment in multicultural settings, very few examined the connection in a Middle Eastern context (A. Cohen, 2006). The need for a more specific understanding of the relationship and development of commitment between differing cultures is important for the success of any organization. It is crucial to understand that theories developed in the context of a certain culture should not then be assumed to be adequate for implementation in another study without analysis (Abdalla & Al-Homoud, 2001; Adler, 1997; Al-Kazemi & Abbas, 2002; Aron, 2006; B. Black, 1999; Boyacigiller & Adler, 1991; Burnett, Williamson, & Bartol, 2009; A. Cohen, 2006; Hofstede, 2007; Meyer & Allen, 1984; Siders, George & Dharwadkar, 2001; Triandis, 2004; Wang, Bishop, Chen, & Scott, 2002).

Hofstede's Model of Cultural Dimensions

Hofstede's model of cultural dimensions is one the most

recognized and accepted cultural dimension models (Adler, 2007;

Askary et al., 2008; Bass, 1990; Fougere & Moulettes, 2006;

Oshlyansky et al., 2006; Triandis, 2004). Hofstede (1980)

developed four dimensions of cultural workplace values and

behaviors and provided in-depth analysis of their implications for

an organization. These four dimensions are power distance,

uncertainty avoidance, masculinity-femininity, and

individualism-collectivism. Hofstede and Bond (1991) added the

dimension of long-term orientation. Later, Minkov and Hofstede

(2011) introduced the dimension of indulgence versus self-

restraint, which gave the model a total of six dimensions.

Power distance refers to the strength of social hierarchy

and the degree a culture tolerates inequality in the distribution of

power (Hofstede, 2001; Hoppe, 1990). This hierarchy is a

determinate in how subordinate and superior behaviors govern

the behavior of the other (Hofstede, 1991). Hofstede (1991)

determined that while all societies have inequality, individuals in a high power distance culture (those with a more centralized

control of power) accept the hierarchical order their respective

position in the society is assigned and do not seek further

justification for the existing hierarchy. In cultures with low

power distance, individuals seek to justify and equalize power

inequalities (Hofstede 1991; Hofstede & Usunier, 1996). Jandt

(2001) determined that power distance has a major influence on

leadership and management styles, negotiation, and decision-

making. Cultures that maintain high power distance are more

likely to use authoritarian leadership and social norms that often

exclude individual members of the culture from the decision-

making process. Conversely, cultures that exhibit low power

distance tend to have relationships between the leadership and the

individual characterized by the concepts of equality,

participation, and empowerment (Hofstede, 2001; Jandt, 2001).

Uncertainty avoidance measures a culture's tolerance for

risk, ambiguity, and the timing and types of actions to reduce

these factors (Hofstede, 2001). A high uncertainty avoidance

rating indicates a culture that is looking to minimize and avoid risk. Decisions are made cautiously and slowly. Authority is the sole component of the decision-making process as control is a crucial factor, and individual empowerment is considered a loss of control. Individuals in a high uncertainty avoidance culture will exhibit higher levels of commitment to the group as the stability of belonging is more highly valued than the instability of being outside of the group (Hofstede, 2001). Low uncertainty avoidance cultures are more likely to take risks, which is exhibited in the individual's position of empowerment in the decision-making process and willingness to take risks for personal advancement (Hofstede, 2001). Jandt (2001) discussed uncertainty avoidance's parallel with power distance and the influence this dimension has on leadership, management styles, negotiation, and decision-making in a culture.

Masculinity-femininity denotes how a culture demonstrates characteristics that have been categorized as being masculine or feminine (Hofstede, 2001). Masculine characteristics represent a culture's level of value for competitiveness, achievement, assertiveness, material rewards for

success, and individualism (Hofstede, 2001). Femininity relates
to the culture's level of value of cooperation, compassion,
modesty, harmony, quality of life for the weak, and consensus
(Hofstede, 2001). B. Black (1999) stated that individuals in a
culture with a high masculine score demonstrate higher levels of
professional commitment but lower levels of group commitment
while individuals in cultures that tend toward a feminine-inclined
culture exhibit the opposite. B. Black and Jandt (2001) reported
that individuals in a high masculine culture participate in a highly
competitive environment wherein status and achievement are
indicators of success. Dedication to a profession as well as a
group is often perceived as a means to attain desired goals and
possessions. Relationships and associations are then viewed as
resources that weaken in value if their perceived usefulness
diminishes (B. Black, 1999; Jandt, 2001).

Individualism-collectivism indicates the degree to which
individuals in a culture define themselves as individuals related
to the larger group (Hofstede, 1980). In high individualistic
cultures individuals are more likely to view their identity separate

from the group. In collectivist cultures individual identity is strongly tied to the group (Hofstede, 1980). Social ties and family structures are more loosely connected in an individualistic culture while the same relationships tend to be integrated in collectivist cultures (Hofstede, 1980). The cultural dimension of individualism versus collectivism is discussed in more detail in the section Collectivism Versus Individualism.

Bond et al. (1987) identified the *Confucian dynamic*, which Hofstede (2001) adapted into the long-term orientation dimension. Hofstede's new dimension is based on Asian perspectives regarding culture and describes a culture's relationship to virtue. As Hofstede (2001) wrote,

> Long Term Orientation stands for the fostering of virtues oriented towards future rewards, in particular perseverance and thrift. Its opposite pole, Short Term Orientation, stands for the fostering of virtues related to the past and present, in particular, respect for tradition, preservation of "face" and fulfilling social obligations. (p. 359)

A culture described as having a long-term orientation dimension fosters an attitude that truth depends on situation, context, and time (Bond et al., 1987; Hofstede, 2001). Long-term orientation indicates cultures able to adapt traditions to current conditions and able to save, invest, and persevere in pursuing goals (Hofstede, 2001). Short-term orientation indicates cultures that exhibit great respect for traditions, that believe in a foundation of an absolute truth, and that exhibit very little ability to save and invest beyond the near future (Hofstede, 2001).

Indulgence versus restraint measures a tendency to allow "relatively free gratification of basic and natural human desires related to enjoying life and having fun. . . . restraint, reflects a conviction that such gratification needs to be curbed and regulated by strict social norms" (Hofstede, Hofstede, & Minkov, 2010, p. 281). Indulgent cultures exhibit a belief in the individual's personal freedoms, a priority on leisure, and have lenient social norms regarding speech and sexuality. A restrained culture exhibits individuals with a sense of helplessness and fatalism, extremely stringent rules concerning speech and sexuality, and often has a high number of police per 100,000 in population (Hofstede et al., 2010, p. 281).

Collectivism Versus Individualism

The role of socioenvironmental cultures in the formation

of self-identity and the development of an individual's daily

thoughts and transactions is extremely powerful (Goffman, 1966;

E. T. Hall, 1992; M. R. Hall & Hall, 1975). Francesco and Gold

(1998) concluded that culture is the predominate factor in

determining how people behave and the most critical component

for gaining understanding and cooperation. B. Black (1999)

determined that culture has a major influence on social values

and norms. Greenfield et al. (2006) stated that a society or

groups can never be completely individualistic or completely

collectivistic but they do develop patterns and preferences that

influence behaviors. Numerous studies have shown culture's

general dimensions as a foundation of a collective set of values

and beliefs that influence behaviors in a society or group

(Hofstede, 1998; House et al., 2004; Mallehi, 2007; Morgan,

1986; Pothukuchi et al., 2002; Schein, 2004; Tayeb, 2005;

Trompenaars & Hamden-Turner, 2000). Further research has

indicated that people of the same national culture are very likely to share similar cognitive frameworks and likely behave in a

similar manner (Alvesson, 2002; Brown, 1995; C. W. L. Hill,

2003; Hofstede, 2001; Kreitner & Kinicki, 1998; Schein, 1995;

Tayeb, 1988).

Some researchers have classified cultures as either

collectivist or individualist societies and stated that these two

dimensions are the most important factors in developing an

understanding of the psychological values that differentiate

nations (Dirani, 2008; Hofstede, 1980, 2001; Hui, Triandis, &

Yee, 1991; Kluckhohn & Strodtbeck, 1961; Triandis, 1988, 1990;

Triandis & Suh, 2002; Trompenaars & Hamden-Turner, 2000).

Collectivism places a greater emphasis on group needs over

individual needs, and individuals are defined in the context of the

larger group (Hofstede, 2001; Triandis, 2004). Identity for

members of a collectivistic culture is derived from the formation

of a group identity, which is strengthened through developing a

high level of interdependence, social responsibility, and

belonging (Greenfield et al., 2006; C. W. L. Hill, 2003). In

collectivistic cultures social hierarchy is often based on gender, birth order, age, and family name (R. S. Black, Mrasek, &

Ballinger, 2003; Lynch, 1998; Triandis, 1995; Trumbull,

Rothstein-Fisch, Greenfield, & Quiroz, 2001); the individual is

defined by the relationship with the group and the conformity,

harmony, and sense of duty displayed to the group (Ellison,

Boykin, Towns, & Stokes, 2000; Green, Deschamps, & Paez,

2005, Triandis, 2004).

The family is of critical importance to a collectivist

culture and often extends beyond the nuclear unit (Greenfield et

al., 2006; Triandis, 1989; Triandis, Brislin, & Hui, 1988). Care

and protection of the family is considered a moral obligation, and

maintaining the family reputation is primary; this would include

discussing family matters or accepting help from outside the

family (Boone, 1992). Family elders' leadership and authority

are unquestioned and provide the model for social authority as

well. Knowledge is considered reserved for elders and leaders,

and it is generally considered disrespectful for children to express

opinions or ask probing questions of their elders. It is expected that knowledge provided is accepted and reflected back (Boone, 1992; C. W. L. Hill, 2003; Triandis, 1984).

Collectivist cultures generally attribute behavior to outside influences and believe that the group is responsible for change within the individual (Triandis, 2004). This dimension emphasizes the expectation that individual members work with and contribute to the group, adhere to traditional values, maintain their position in the social hierarchy, and fulfill their expected roles (Ellison et al., 2000; Green et al., 2005, Triandis, 2004). This dimension also fosters a very sharp distrust and resistance to knowledge and change from outside the group (Green et al., 2005; C. W. L. Hill, 2003; Hofstede, 2001; Triandis, 2004)

Communication and interaction norms vary a great deal across cultures. Although all cultures share the concept that appropriateness depends on social status (Bhawuk & Brislin, 1992; Ellingsworth, 1983), collectivistic cultures generally expect those of lower social status to observe defined decorum when communicating with those of higher social rank (Green et al., 2005; Hofstede, 2007; Triandis, 2004). Collectivist cultures value context over content in communication and place a high

value on the subtle nuances of the historical, situational, and

relational context surrounding the topic (Thomas & Osland,

2004). The high value of relationship over outcome also

influences communication; direct, explicit communication may

be interpreted as rude and insulting (Bhawuk & Brislin, 1992;

Ellingsworth, 1983; Thomas & Osland, 2004).

Individualism generally displays the attributes of

independence, competition, achievement, uniqueness, and

individual self-reliance and an emphasis on individuals obtaining

satisfaction of their personal needs (Green et al., 2005; Triandis,

2004). The individual is defined as a separate unit of society and

is measured by the level of contribution, achievement, and status

(Hofstede, 2001; Triandis, 2004). Nonconformity and exclusion

from the ingroup can be valued and admired as there is an

emphasis on self-expression (Black, 1990). Individualistic

cultures promote the belief that the society is made stronger

through the independent success/achievements of each member

and that each member of the society has certain rights that may not be violated or infringed upon by other individuals or the

society as a whole (Black, 1990; Green et al., 2005; Hofstede,

2007; Triandis, 2004).

The family is also important to the individualistic society,

and the position of the elders as leaders is respected.

Expectations of children are that they should develop and assume

the role of decision-making for themselves. Adult members of an

individualistic society are expected to be self-sufficient, define

their personal values, and determine their role in the social

context (Black, 1990; Green et al., 2005; Hofstede, 2007;

Triandis, 2004). To a member of an individualistic society,

family is viewed as a support system, but reliance and request for

such support is often believed to be a last resort and a burden one

prefers to not impose (Boone, 1992; C. W. L. Hill, 2003). Honor

is brought to the family through individual accomplishment and

status, and children are encouraged to seek knowledge and

develop and express opinions (Boone, 1992; C. W. L. Hill, 2003;

Hofstede, 2007; Triandis, 2004). In individualistic cultures

information and knowledge being readily available to all

members of the society for their self-advancement is a highly

regarded value (Black, 1990; Green et al., 2005; Hofstede, 2007;

Triandis, 2004).

In individualistic cultures communication can often be

impersonal and linked to time management and production. The

distinction between personal and business relationships can often

give the context of a relationship being a vehicle for gain or

advancement (Bhawuk & Brislin, 1992; Ellingsworth, 1983;

Thomas & Osland, 2004). Directly addressing topics or issues,

providing personal opinions, and questioning for clarity are

considered proper and acceptable communication (Bhawuk &

Brislin, 1992; Ellingsworth, 1983; Thomas & Osland, 2004). In

an individualistic culture, relationship is considered of high value

but outcome and time as a resource often merit a higher value,

which is a different nuance to be observed in communication

(Bhawuk & Brislin, 1992; Ellingsworth, 1983; Thomas &

Osland, 2004).

Black (1980) characterized the importance of the

individual making decisions and judgments on the perceived

value to the group. In a collectivist culture individuals and the

ingroup have a moral obligation to care and provide for each

other (Black, 1990; Haslberger, 2008; Hofstede, 2001; Triandis,

2004). In individualistic cultures, members are ultimately

responsible for their behavior and outcomes. This often puts

relationships in the context of an investment. If the member

comes to believe the costs exceed the advantages then the

relationship could terminate (Haslberger, 2008; Thomas &

Osland, 2004).

Researchers have defined the Arab culture as being

collectivist (Ali, Taqi & Krishnan, 1997; At-Twaijri & Al-

Muhaiza, 1996; Dirani, 2008; Klein, Waxin, & Radnell, 2009),

demonstrating very high levels of commitment to the group

structures of immediate family, extended family, and the work

group. At-Twaijri and Al-Muhaiza (1996) reported that

individuals within the society identify a distinction between the

ingroup (relatives, clans, and tribes) and others with a distrust of

outsiders. Bjerke and Al-Meer (1993) measured national culture

values using Hofstede's culture dimensions and reported that, when compared to the United States, Arab culture scored

considerably higher on power distance and uncertainty avoidance

but considerably lower on individualism and masculinity.

Culture Shock

Individuals who begin expatriate assignments often find

that adjusting to the new cultural context is a daily challenge

(Black et al., 1991; Brien & David, 1971; Church, 1982; Early &

Ang, 2003; Furnham, 1988; Mendenhall & Oddou, 1985;

Newman & Nollen, 1996). The phenomenon of culture shock

was initially researched by Oberg (1954, 1960), who designed the

model of culture shock commonly cited in expatriate literature.

Oberg's model is simplistic and presents a clear and easy way to

understand the adjustment period related to the emotional

experience and physical discomfort individuals may experience

when they find themselves adjusting to a new culture. Oberg

identified the process as consisting of four stages: honeymoon,

crisis/culture shock, adjustment/recovery, and adaptation.

The honeymoon stage (Oberg, 1960) is when individuals

experience emotions of wonder, excitement, fascination, and

enthusiasm regarding the new environment. Differences are considered exhilarating as the period is marked by observation and discoveries. During this phase any warnings of potential developing issues of adjustment can be masked, minimized, and discounted. There is also a danger that unrealistic expectations can be formulated.

The crisis or cultural shock stage (Oberg, 1960) is defined as when individuals begin to struggle with the nuances of the host culture. As individuals interact more with the new culture, difficulties in understanding the culture's idiosyncrasies can result in frustration, criticism, resentment, and anger. Developing feelings of dislike for the new culture may lead to unfair comparisons to the home culture. The emergence of additional emotions of anxiety, homesickness, loneliness, self-doubt, and feelings of being overwhelmed can lead to withdrawal from the new culture and thoughts of returning to the individual's home culture environment. The greatest risk factors are often found in subtle nuances of the new culture that compound and create the expatriate's aggregate feeling of being overwhelmed. The inability to maintain effective social communication becomes a major issue. Feelings of lack of understanding and frustrations in gathering information coupled with any unrealistic expectations established during the honeymoon period can create a level of disillusionment that may lead to completely rejecting the new culture. Emotions of rejection can influence emotions concerning the new work assignment which, when associated with the change, can resentment and disengagement and lead to returning to the home culture.

The adjustment or recovery stage (Oberg, 1960) is characterized by individuals developing a series of routines in which the cultural nuances have become more familiar. It is also marked by a sense of improved communication. This period also is often associated with individuals feeling they have stronger support systems. Honeymoon stage elements that may resurface as this stage could be described as an oscillation between the two first stages, from renewed feelings of excitement to bouts of frustration and depression.

Lastly, the adaptation stage (Oberg, 1960) finds individuals working in familiar patterns with a sense of established background from the new culture. They have developed a working understanding of the similarities and differences between the two cultures and adopted coping mechanisms for adaptation essential for adjustment. Individuals in this stage may have even developed a sense of feeling at home by identifying elements of the new culture they enjoy as well as certain behaviors of the new culture they have adopted as their own. It is important to note that the cycle may repeat itself many times during the expatriate's tenure. The duration and magnitude of each occurrence can vary with no set timeframe of pattern of occurrence as each experience is as unique as the individual expatriate.

Several researchers have identified the role of subtle nuances and the individual's ability to identify and cope as crucial factors in expatriate failure (Lee & Croker, 2006; Rose, Ramalu, Uli, & Kumar, 2010). Haslberger (2005) argued that expatriate adjustment is also significantly "influenced by environmental factors" (p. 86) such as Hofstede's (2001) cultural

distance as well as "surprises that develop within the new

context; social networks; and organizational support" (p. 87).

According to Black and Gregersen (1997), culture shock

is a "stress induced by all the behavioral expectation differences

and the accompanying uncertainty with which the individual

must cope" (p. 672). Black et al. (1991) discussed the disruption

of familiar routines and psychological securities as factors in

culture shock. Solomon (1994) described the "emotional and

psychological reactions to the confusion, ambiguity, value

conflicts, and hidden clashes that occur as a result of

fundamentally different ways of perceiving the world and

interacting socially between cultures: Disequilibrium" (p. 58).

Researchers have generally agreed that not all adaptations

are equal, and some cultural differences may be more difficult to

adapt to than others (termed *cultural distance*; Gilbert & Tsao,

2000; Kupka, Everett, & Cathro, 2008; Lee & Croker, 2006;

Rose et al., 2010). More recent researchers have targeted specific

psychological and emotional functions within the stages model of culture shock. These researchers have examined psychological process theories of adjustment (Javidan et al., 2006; Maertz et al., 2009; Molinsky, 2007; Van Vianen et al., 2004). Tsui, Nifadkar, and Ou (2007) discussed adjustment using the terms acculturation and adaptation. Maertz et al. (2009) described a cultural cognitive dissonance reduction model based on the theory that an expatriate's values, attitudes, beliefs, or behavioral norms (VABNs) create an internal conflict for the expatriate that signals the end of the honeymoon stage and the emergence of the next stage in the cycle. This conflict is the struggle in reconciling perceived culturally appropriate behaviors with the expatriate's VABNs.

Examining for causes and elements of effect concerning culture shock, Jacoby, Nason, and Saguchi (2005) suggested that factors influencing culture shock can be classified into two categories: internal/individual factors, which constitute elements of psychological well-being, self-efficacy, empathy, cognitive flexibility, ethics, values, communication style, motivation, and family situation; and external/organizational factors, which relate to organizational size, complexity, management style, culture,

labor practices, training programs, and support programs; and

product market pressures. Malie and Akir (2012) suggested that

flexibility/adaptability, motivation, family situation, and

extracultural openness significantly impact the severity of the

culture shock cycle as well as the expatriate employee's ability to

adjust.

Expatriate Failure

Expatriate assignments for multinational corporations

declined during the 2008 worldwide economic downturn (Batt &

Colvin, 2011). Data trends in the first three quarters of 2011

suggested that the number of expatriate assignments increased in

response to economic recovery and continued emphasis on a

global business expansion (Batt & Colvin, 2011). Researchers

have determined that 10% to 80% (the wide range encompasses a

large variance as specific job sectors and geographic regions

greatly vary in their respective rates) of all expatriates will

experience expatriate failure in the form of resignation, transfer,

or return to their home country prior to completing their

commitment (Peltokorpi & Froese, 2011). Another aspect of failure is demonstrated when expatriates remain but display tendencies of underperforming in their assignments and become ineffectively disengaged (Black & Mendenhall, 1989; K. Kim & Slocum, 2008; Mendenhall, Dunbar, & Oddou, 1987). According to Brookfield Global Relocation Services (2010), 38% of returnees quit within the first 12 months of the assignment.

An expatriate's failure can be very costly and time consuming. Tziner and Birati (1996) calculated that replacement costs amounted to approximately 150% of annual base salary while Dube, Freeman, and Reich (2010) found the level can vary between 150% to 250% of annual base salary excluding lost productivity. Batt and Colvin (2011) cited the most recent cost estimate of expatriate assignments to total between $2,000,000,000 and $2,500,000,000 USD per year. Indirect costs, not all of which are overtly financial, are also associated with failed assignments (Hechanova, Beehr, & Christiansen, 2003; McDonald, 1993; Stierle, van Dick, & Wagner, 2002). In addition to lost revenue and productivity, expatriate failure can have a negative effect on the remaining employees' perceptions of the organization as well as organization's ability to recruit top talent for new positions (Bennett, Aston, & Colquhoun, 2000; Black & Gregersen, 1991; Stierle et al., 2002).

Expatriates can also suffer loss as a result of assignment failures. OEs and SIEs risk psychological consequences such as loss of self-esteem, self-confidence, prestige, and motivation (Hechanova et al., 2003; McDonald, 1993; Mendenhall & Oddou, 1985; Mendenhall et al., 1987; Takeuchi, Yun, & Tesluk, 2002; Tung, 1988). Expatriates' families may also suffer from the psychological consequences experienced by the expatriate as well as negative emotions and anxieties of their own (J. E. Harris, 1989; Schneider & Asakawa, 1995). SIEs often face severe personal economic loss as they do not have an organization to cover costs associated with relocation, health care, education, and residency (Chen, 2012; Fermelis, 2011; Fitzgerald & Howe-Walsh, 2008).

Conceptualizing Expatriate Assignment Failure and Success

The most common identifier of expatriate assignment failure or success is whether or not an expatriate returns home before the completion of the defined assignment period (Black, 1988, Black & Gregersen, 1990; Caligiuri & Colakoglu, 2007; Tung, 1981). Researchers who examined production, performance, and commitment levels defined this criterion as the most viable point of reference for determining an assignment outcome (Aycan, 1997; Birdseye & Hill, 1995; Kraimer & Wayne, 2004; Naumann, 1993; Shaffer et al., 2006). H. W. Lee (2007) argued this definition's inadequacies, and Peng (2009) concluded that the continuing high rates of turnover required further study. Mol et al. (2005) stated that the ambiguity of an assignment success definition must be settled before the gap between research and practice can be bridged.

Forster (1997) and later Bossard and Peterson (2005) stated that success/failure evaluation was extremely biased from the organization's perspective but little data existed regarding the expatriates' perspectives. Bossard and Peterson explored

returned expatriates' attitudes regarding their willingness to
accept another expatriate assignment. The results were mixed,
but Bossard and Peterson noted that positive experiences
typically related to willingness to accept another assignment
while negative experiences related to an unwillingness to accept
an assignment. Bossard and Peterson suggested further research
on perceptions of the experience as they relate to success.

Why Expatriates Fail

Digman (1990) and McCrae and Costa (1987) developed
the Big Five personality or five-factor model. This inventory
identifies and categorizes personality traits using the following
classifications: "conscientiousness, emotional stability,
agreeableness, openness to experience, and extraversion"
(Digman, 1990, p. 415; McCrae & Costa, 1987, pp. 82–83).
These five factors can be aligned to identify traits that will
positively and negatively impact individuals immersed in
unfamiliar cultures. Other researchers have suggested that these
elements may influence expatriate success (Black & Gregersen,

1991; Harrison & Shaffer, 2005; Mendenhall & Oddou, 1985, 1991; Shafer et al., 1999).

Caligiuri (2000a) determined that personality traits are relatively stable and that measuring these traits can predict responses to stress. Berry (1997) identified an adjustment process that included the expatriate's feelings of comfort, level of control, and the degree of perceived familiarity regarding the host culture. Sinangil and Ones (2001) examined how these factors affected reactions and behaviors related to the acculturative stress expatriates feel.

Brandl and Neyer (2009) discussed the concept of cognitive adjustment in the context of sensemaking theory and examined how individuals changed their mindsets through interaction with the host culture. Maertz et al. (2009) proposed that sensemaking and adjustment could be easier if the individuals develop a strategy or method of dissonance reduction. Brandl and Neyer (2009) and Maertz et al. (2009) all stated that cross-cultural training could help individuals adjust faster. Javidan et al. (2006) discussed how conflicts in values can create an identity crisis and that not all personality types are capable of

adjustment. Research results suggest that individuals who

understand the specific risk factors concerning their own

vulnerability to culture shock may be better prepared to make

choices concerning expatriate assignments. They also suggest

that organizations looking to assign expatriate workers can design

more effective training programs to support these workers

(Brandl & Neyer, 2009; Harrison & Shaffer, 2005; Javidan et al.,

2006; Maertz et al., 2009; Mendenhall & Oddou, 1991).

Expatriate employees represent a high investment for

organizations that employ them. Traditionally, the burden for

adjustment has fallen upon the expatriates themselves, and few if

any support programs have been developed to help expatriates

understand and adjust to the subtle nuances of their new

environment. Tung (1982) stated that parent organizations often

used expatriate assignment to develop and maintain the

organization's corporate culture. With this goal in mind,

retention was viewed as linked to compensation and prestige.

Past success was considered a key factor in predicting expatriate assignment success (Gupta & Govindarajan, 1991; Tung, 1981, 1987, 1988, 2004; Varner, 2002).

Several researchers have identified the role of subtle nuances and the individual's ability to identify and cope as crucial factors in expatriate success (Lee & Croker, 2006; Rose & Kumar, 2008). Haslberger (2005) argued that expatriate adjustment is also significantly "influenced by environmental factors" (p. 86) such as Hofstede's (2001) cultural distance. Adjustment is also affected by "surprises that develop within the new context; social networks; and organizational support" (Haslberger, 2005, p. 87). Organizations can contribute to expatriate adjustment by using appropriate methods to select expatriate workers who display the identified natural abilities to adjust. Organizations can also provide comprehensive training programs including pre- and postdeparture programs for educating expatriates on identifying these subtle differences and for coping with them. Organizations must also include the family unit in trainings, clearly define role and performance expectations, and provide adequate support services for the

duration of the expatriate's assignment (Andreason, 2003).

Adjustment

Adjustment has been defined as "the degree of

psychological adjustment experienced by the individual within a

new society or the degree of psychological comfort and

familiarity perceived within a new environment" (Puck, Mohr, &

Rygl, 2008, p. 2). Researchers have conceived adjustment as

involving three domains: general living adjustment, interaction

adjustment, and work adjustment (Black, 1988; Black &

Stephens, 1989; Gregersen & Black, 1990; Huang et al., 2005;

Nicholson, 1984; Oberg, 1960). Bhaskar-Shrinivas et al. (2005)

conducted a meta-analytic review of 66 studies. Results

supported the three domain theories and suggested that additional

extensions should be incorporated in the theory. Blakeney (2006)

stated that psychological adjustment and sociocultural adaptation

are separate but related constructs that function in the outcome of

an expatriate assignment. Haslberger and Brewster (2007)

argued that while the domains may be valid, an expatriate may

85

experience several roles within each domain, thus requiring a more specified measurement of domain components. Haslberger and Brewster distinguished six domains based on the work of Navas et al. (2005, 2007). Navas et al. (2005, 2007) defined the following domains and ordered them by the level of increasing resistance to change for the individual experiencing the adjustment:

1. politics and government,

2. work,

3. economics,

4. social relationships,

5. family relationships, and

6. ideology, which has two distinct divisions: ways of thinking, principles and values; and religious beliefs and customs.

According to Navas et al. (2007), "The division into domains of acculturation provides a richer, more precise perspective of the way in which immigrants face their own acculturation process, compared to the classical models" (p. 83).

Haslberger and Brewster (2007) argued that the order ranking of increasing resistance to adjustment by domain implies that adjustment may happen at different speeds for individuals. Haslberger and Brewster also suggested that this is supported by the realm of underlying assumptions as developed by Schein (1985). Tams and Arthur (2007) stated that while OEs and SIEs may in principle apply the defined concept of adjustment it is reasonable to expect that adjustment's process, determinants, and outcomes differ significantly between the groups given the differences in the context between the two groups.

Domains of Adjustment

Navas et al.'s (2007) first domain of adjustment is politics and government. Navas et al. did not suggest that immigrants become involved in the host country's political activities. Politics and government also refer to the overt systems of public order such as laws and regulations. Adjustment within the domain of politics and government is simply learning and accepting how to act and behave. This domain is considered the one requiring the least amount of time and change for an individual.

The work domain, according to Navas et al. (2005, 2007), is most associated with performance, task completion, and work-beneficial relationships. Navas et al. and Haslberger and Brewster (2007) believed this domain to be underdeveloped and that it may significantly spill over into other domains. Haslberger and Brewster suggested that stress and tension one experiences at work as well as coping mechanisms and relationships one develops influence one's reactions and level of adjustment in the other domains. Haslberger and Brewster also suggested that personality and family structure play intricate parts in the work domain. Even with this complexity, work often has a built-in support system and the individual has a foundation of past experience and competency to rely upon, which is why this domain is placed in the second position in terms of resistance to adjustment.

The economics domain includes "sharing goods produced, economic transactions and consumer habits: e.g., items purchased, money spent and saved, ways of managing income, etc." (Navas et al. 2005, p. 28). Economics can create a level of discomfort. Gilly (1995) discussed how simple routines an individual develops are often found to be hindrances; minor needs such as learning new ways of shopping for goods, meal and services timing, and regulations and procedures for completing transactions become stressful and sources of conflict that affect perceptions and judgments regarding other domains in the new culture.

The social relations domain is unique and separated from the routine of day-to-day activities. According to Navas et al. (2005, 2007), social relations is the process and establishment of networks, contacts, and friendships. Navas et al. and Haslberger and Brewster (2007) suggested that these are central components to Olberg's (1960) culture shock. Navas et al. found that immigrants developed and maintained a separation strategy whereby the individual's home culture approach to forming social relationships remained intact. Haslberger and Brewster contended that expatriates will also display this pattern and tend to form expatriate subcultures for social interaction.

Navas et al. (2005, 2007) discussed how family structure dynamics have a spillover influence as the family confronts issues such as schooling for the children, acceptable parenting roles and behaviors, public appearances, and acceptable gender roles within the host culture. Haslberger and Brewster (2007) reported that most expatriate research has not designated familial relations as a separate domain, which negates the inclusion of work-family/family-work conflict as an influence in expatriate adjustment.

Navas et al.'s (2005, 2007) sixth domain is that of ideology (culture). This domain is divided into two subdomains of ways of thinking, principles, and values and religious beliefs and customs. Navas et al. agreed with Hofstede (1980), House et al. (2004) and Trompenaars (1993) that ideology was the hub of operationalization of culture. Navas et al. also agreed with Schein (1985) that as this domain is rooted in the deepest layer of the home culture and entangled with the individual's concept of identity, it would be the most difficult to adjust to because people would be least likely to want to change at this level.

Spillover Between Domains

Navas et al. (2005, 2007) discussed and Haslberger and

Brewster (2007) further developed the concept of spillover or

linkages between domains. These linkages may be found in the

areas of behavioral, cognitive, or affective dimension.

Haslberger and Brewster discussed how experiences and changes

made in one domain may spill over into adjustment in another

domain. These influences could be either positive or negative

and may act as either an enhancement or a restraint of

adjustment. Haslberger and Brewster also noted that domains

may not have equal importance and acknowledged that, because

of personality differences, the salience of each domain may vary

between individuals. Lastly, Haslberger and Brewster also listed

the differences between host and home culture characteristics as a

variable.

GCC Issues

This section includes an introduction of GCC countries

and a discussion of the specific issues that results in the unique

situations for expatriates living and working in these countries.

The GCC was founded on May 26, 1981, and consists of the nations of Bahrain, Kuwait, Saudi Arabia, Qatar, the Sultanate of Oman, and the UAE. The GCC countries share common a common culture and history and are further tied together by the common language of Arabic, a heavily Bedouin tradition, and Islam as the official state religion. The GCC was formed to promote economic development, social reform, and policy coordination between member states in order to achieve unity and economic power (Al-Kazemi & Abbas, 2002; Hassan, 2013). This union has resulted in all six countries employing similar regulations concerning immigration, social reforms, economic investment, education, tourism, and legislative administration (Al-Bawaba, 2012; Al-Rasheedi, 2012; Al-Waqfi, 2012).

The GCC countries comprise several of the fastest growing economies in the world based on 36.7% of the world's total crude oil and natural gas reserves and rapidly expanding investment in alternative power generation, telecommunications, tourism, and real estate (Datamatrix, 2013). The economic crisis of 2008 encouraged the GCC's acceleration of economic diversification measures, and investment in educational reforms became a key focus in the move from depending on petroleum and natural gas revenues to a more tourism- and knowledge-based economy (Datamatrix, 2013; Rehman, 2008).

GCC revenues from the petroleum industry have influenced the implementation of major infrastructure projects and created a severe qualified workforce shortage in many areas. The shortage of a local qualified workforce has in turn led the GCC to rely heavily on a workforce composed of SIEs. It has been estimated that the percentage of expatriates in the GCC workforce is as high as 90% in some of the GCC countries with the areas of education, medicine, and finance most heavily relying on SIEs (Al-Bawaba, 2012; Al-Waqfi, 2012). While a high percentage of this workforce comes from other areas of the Arab world and the subcontinent of India, the past decade has seen a major increase in the number of Western SIEs (Al-Rasheedi, 2012; International Labour Organization, 2013).

One of the major factors that contributed to this increase
is massive educational reform with plans for developing a
comprehensive education system for boys and girls composed of
governmental schools, private schools, colleges, and universities
(International Labour Organization, 2013). It is estimated the
number of SIEs entering the GCC countries in 2013 was over
4,500,000 with an estimated 20% employed in educational or
related sectors (Al-Rasheedi, 2012; International Labour
Organization, 2013). Until the discovery of oil, the GCC had a
closed nature. The fundamental introversion of the culture
coupled with the rapid growth and influx of foreign workers
created the dilemma of a local workforce that is unaccustomed to
understanding cultural differences and an expatriate workforce
that does not understand its influence on rapidly changing
domestic environment (Al-Rasheedi, 2012).

The Islamic Religion and Work Values

Religion is one of the most predominate influencers in the
shaping of national culture (Hickson & Pugh, 1995; P. C. Hill,
2005; Hofstede, 2001; Mencil, 2005; Rice, 2003). Islam

permeates every area of life in the GCC region, imprinting and

defining the national culture (Lundgren, 1998; Mababaya, 2002;

Moran, Harris, & Moran, 2007; Nydell, 2012; Rehman, 2008;

Rice, 2003; Williams, 2010). This influence is experienced in

every level of business and in the function and structure of

organizations within the GCC (Ali, 1995; Mababaya, 2002;

Nydell, 2012; Rehman, 2008; Rice, 2003; Williams, 2010). Two

specific areas of conflict for Western expats can be found in

personal responsibility and time management (Nydell, 2012;

Rehman, 2008; Rice, 2003; Williams, 2010).

Islam teaches that individuals are obligated to have an

obligation to take initiative over the aspects of their lives but are

also to believe that ultimate control lies in the hand of God. As

such, there is a level of applied sense of fatalism in which

individuals often blame fate rather than take responsibility for

poor outcomes in results or organizational systems (Bhuiyan,

Paul, & Jabber, 2002; Nydell, 2012; F. Walker, Walker, &

Schmitz, 2003). This same fatalism is applied to time

management. A popular Arab idiom "There is something good in

95

every delay" (Williams, 2010) indicates the tolerance for unexpected delays, but while things tend to move very slowly in the GCC there is a propensity to demand periods of intense work against impossible deadlines (Bhuiyan et al., 2002; Nydell, 2012; Rehman, 2008; F. Walker et al., 2003; Williams, 2010). Both the Koran and the Sunnah (the sayings and practices of the Prophet Mohammad) give specific instruction in many areas of ethical standards and business practices that all Muslims are expected to adhere without deviation (Bhuiyan et al., 2002; Mababaya, 2002; Nydell, 2012; Rehman, 2008; F. Walker et al., 2003; Williams, 2010). Islam's tenets regarding all business arrangements require a documented and formalized agreement in which both parties are expected to honor the employer-employee relationship (Bhuiyan et al., 2002; 2010; Mababaya, 2002; Nydell, 2012; Rehman, 2008; F. Walker et al., 2003; Williams, 2010).

In Islamic Arab culture, the employer/leader is seen as a father figure who is responsible for his employees/subordinates, success, and welfare (Bhuiyan et al., 2002, 2010; Kalliny, Cruthirds & Minor, 2006; Nydell, 2012; Rehman, 2008;

Williams, 2010). Employees/subordinates are expected to adhere to all directives from the leader; the only exception allowed would be a directive that does not align with Islam's tenets (Abdalla & Al-Homoud, 2001; Denny, 2005; Kalliny et al., 2006; Nydell, 2012; Rehman, 2008; Williams, 2010). This paternalistic managerial style encourages Arab employees to expect working conditions to be safe and fair and encourages a reluctance to oppose or question superiors (Abdalla & Al-Homoud, 2001; Kalliny et al., 2006; Nydell, 2012; Rehman, 2008; Williams, 2010). Leaders are expected to exemplify Islamic principles of fairness and forgiveness, which in ideal circumstances leads to an environment based on mutual respect and commitment but also allows for an environment founded in fear (Abdalla & Al-Homoud, 2001).

Business in the Arab culture is also considered as a personal interaction with a hierarchy of family and Muslims first, then strangers second (Nydell, 2012; Williams, 2010). Developing trust becomes crucial, and it is developed through a combination of business and pleasure displayed with a consistent behavior and etiquette as bargaining and negotiating are both viewed as serious and a game (Nydell, 2012; Williams, 2010). In the Arab culture, a person's word is taken to be as good as a written commitment because the Koran states that it is a moral obligation for a man to keep his word (Kalliny et al., 2006; Mababaya, 2002; Nydell, 2012; Rice, 2003). It is critical in communication for one to be aware of how a position and intention is stated; casual comments of intention can be a source of conflict as it is culturally unacceptable and considered a religious sin for an individual not to do what was promised (Kalliny et al., 2006; Mababaya, 2002; Nydell, 2012; Rice, 2003).

Bedouin Traditions

Hofstede (2007) reported on the influence of the cultural values and shared attitudes in forming a national identity and also identified the differences from one area of the world to another. Badawy (1980) and Yavas and Yasin (1999) discussed how an understanding of cultural and social characteristics can enhance the expatriate experience. The interconnected factors of religion,

98

the tribal historical heritage, and strong family traditions are major influences in Arab culture (Abu-Laghod, 2000; R. R. Andersen, Siebert & Wagner, 2007; Keohane, 2003).

The Arab Bedouin heritage also has a tremendous influence on the formation of national identity (Abu-Laghod, 2000; R. R. Andersen et al., 2007; Kalliny et al., 2006). The historical background of the Bedouin, or desert dweller, is that of a nomadic people who covered a range from the Arabian Gulf to the border of Turkey, from Yemen throughout North Africa from Sudan to Morocco (Abu-Laghod, 2000; R. R. Andersen et al., 2007; Keohane, 2003). The Bedouin developed a strong code of justice and systems of hospitality-generosity, honor-dignity, and courage-bravery that predate Islam but were deeply reinforced by Islam's introduction (Patai, 2001).

Hospitality-generosity had a practical application as its development was directly related to the hardships and struggles of the nomadic desert life, which increased the importance of communication and information as a valuable and scarce commodity (Abu-Laghod, 2000; R. R. Andersen et al., 2007;

Kalliny et al., 2006; Patai, 2001). In contrast to Western emphasis on the oral component of communication, traditional Bedouin communication places a strong emphasis on the aural component of listening, which benefited the group as a whole in network and association development (Moran et al., 2007). Islam also added an increased emphasis of hospitality-generosity as an element of status and honor for the individual, the family, and the group (Kalliny et al., 2006). The final component is related to the collectivist attitude of redistribution of prosperity and other resources for the betterment of the society (Kalliny et al., 2006; Patai, 2001).

Honor-dignity is founded in group survival as it reinforces cohesion conducive to group survival while dishonorable behavior tends to weaken the social collectiveness (Abu-Laghod, 2000; Patai, 2001). Bedouin tradition attaches individual actions of dishonor to the entire family and/or group (Patai, 2001). Honor-dignity is considered the most important factor in building relationships that characterize all business and professional relationships (Lundgren, 1998; Moran et al., 2007).

Courage-bravery is defined as the willingness of an

individual to defend one's group or tribe. Courage-bravery is

also a key component of *muruwa* or the individual's level of

manliness (Abu-Laghod, 2000). These tribal codes are the legacy

upon which Bedouin heritage builds family structure, social

order, and the business culture (Abu-Laghod, 2000; Ali, 1995;

Hickson & Pugh, 1995; Kalliny et al., 2006; Kassem & Habib,

1989; Rice, 2003; Tayeb, 2005).

Implications

Islamic rules and values coupled with Bedouin tradition

form the foundational mechanisms of modern Arab society in the

GCC region (Abu-Laghod, 2000; Kassem & Habib, 1989).

Anderson, Hubona, and Al-Gahtani (2007) identified the

following areas as areas of major difference between GCC Arab

and Western human resource practices: the employment, status,

and treatment of women; managerial practices regarding the

leader/subordinate relationship; and the common practice of

nepotism and favoritism). Moran et al. (2007) and Niblock and

Malik (2007) identified how these cultural norms can have a

negative impact on female expatriates who find work in the region as well as female family members who accompany expatriate spouses.

Summary

Chapter II was an overview of the research regarding the phenomenon of expatriation, the emergence of SIEs, and current theories of expatriate adjustment. An examination of the models of culture and culture shock and their roles in expatriate adjustment was also presented. Research findings have indicated a gap in knowledge concerning the understanding of expatriate adjustment. Maslow (1954) determined that an individual's basic foundational needs are physiological but that intricate connections to the psychological exist. The continued growth of global mobility and the increasing numbers of those who seek to expatriate themselves have brought into focus the lack of academic research on SIEs' experiences regarding the phenomenon of displacement and relocation. There is a need for greater understanding of the elements and factors that contribute to the prospects of failure and success for the SIE. What are the experiences that create the most difficulty in the process of the

psychological and social sensemaking? Do these experiences

influence behavioral and value adjustments for the SIE?

Researchers have yet to establish a comprehensive depiction of

the process of expatriate adjustment. There is a need to examine

the specific domains of the adjustment process. What research

that does exist is predominately geared to the OE, with research

concerning the recent phenomenon of SIEs being extremely

limited (Doherty, Dickmann, & Mills, 2011; Fitzgerald & Howe-

Walsh, 2008; Jokinen, Brewster, & Sutari, 2008). Chapter II

provided the foundation for the current study and its focus on

examining the phenomenon of SIE adjustment. It was hoped that

the present study would contribute to the body of literature

concerning adjustment for SIEs, specifically in the GCC.

CHAPTER III: RESEARCH METHODOLOGY

The present study was exploratory with a focus on investigating SIEs' perceptions and feelings during their adjustment to working and living in the GCC region. As stated in Chapter I, much research has been conducted on the factors contributing to expatriate failure, the majority focused on the OEs. Prior researchers have stated that the inability to adjust can be attributed to the disorientation between the expatriate's values and beliefs and what the expatriate perceives as appropriate behavior in the new cultural environment (Black, 1988; Jovian et al., 2006; Maertz et al., 2009; Molinsky, 2007; Van Vianen et al., 2004). Yin (2003) stated that three conditions best determine the appropriate research strategy to employ. The first condition to be considered is the type of research question, the second should be how much control the researcher has over behavioral events, and the final condition is the degree of focus on contemporary as opposed to historical events (Yin, 2003, p. 5).

Applying Yin's (2003) conditions to the current study determined that the best method for addressing this study's purpose and research question would be a qualitative approach as this approach would allow using various data collection techniques, such as semistructured interviews and documentary analysis, to explore concepts and gather data on SIEs' perceptions of their abilities to live and work in a culturally diverse environment. Qualitative research was deemed more suitable than quantitative research as it allowed for what Snape and Spencer (2003) defined as the "'emic' perspective, i.e. analyzing the self-perception on that subject of people under study" (p. 4).

Smith, Flowers, and Larkin's (2009) IPA approach was deemed as the appropriate methodology for exploring the meaning and experience of expatriate adjustment in the capacity of an SIE. Chapter III contains a description and justification of IPA methodology as an appropriate application to gain an understanding of "the perspective of the person or persons being studied" (Willis, 2007, p. 107). A discussion of the chosen methods of data collection and data analysis follows with justification for using digitally recorded, semistructured interviews to gather data and using IPA techniques for data

coding and analysis. Issues related to reliability, ethics, and

ensuring trustworthiness through establishing researcher

positioning and appropriate documentation are also discussed in

detail. The chapter includes the following sections: research

design strategy, methodology selected, study participant

selection, data collection, data analysis, procedures,

trustworthiness, and ethical concerns.

Research Design Appropriateness

Neuman (2006) discussed quantitative method structure

involving deductive and linear direction that requires the

researcher to be distinct from the subjects as the analysis focuses

on the relationships and results between specific variables.

Quantitative methods rely on hard, measurable data that can be

objectively generalized while limiting the researcher's scope of

exploration of the participants' lived experiences (Simon, 2006).

As the focus of the present study was on exploring the meaning

of the experiences of SIE educators in the GCC, a qualitative

approach, specifically phenomenology, was the appropriate

methodology (Briscoe et al., 2006; Dickmann & Harris, 2005;

Kollinger, 2007; Moustakas, 1994; Richardson, 2006).

Qualitative methodology does not assume there is a single or

objective reality to be uncovered but instead guides data

collection and analysis techniques by clustering raw data into

sub- and superordinate themes to build a detailed picture of the

phenomenon in question (Smith, 2004, 2007).

Data were collected by conducting semistructured, in-

depth interviews. IPA was used to engage with individuals and

explore their sensemaking of lived experiences. Qualitative IPA

research is an appropriate application to gain an understanding of

"the perspective of the person or persons being studied" (Willis,

2007, p. 107) through the detailed description of those who

concretely lived the phenomenon (Giorgi, 2008; Hegel, 1977;

Heidegger, 1962; Husserl, 1970; van Manen, 1990; Wertz, 2005).

IPA (Smith et al., 2009) explores the sensemaking of the

participant's personal and social worlds based on the meanings

particular events hold for the participant. IPA allows the

researcher an active role in trying to obtain what Conrad (1987) termed an insider's perspective through recording the

participant's experience and then interpreting that experience as it

applies to the participant. IPA does not seek to make objective

statements about the event itself (Smith et al., 2009). IPA is thus

considered a two-stage interpretive process: the participant

making sense of the experience and the researcher trying to make

sense of the participant's sensemaking process.

IPA allows the researcher to attempt to understand the

participant's perspective through critically questioning the

narrative. According to Smith et al. (2009), when dealing with

adjustment, the questions people ask denote the reality of their

experiences. Answers to such questions as "What is happening

here?" and "Is the outcome intended or desired?" as well as the

research questions "Is the information the participant sharing

unintended?" and "To what extent is the participant aware of

what is happening during the event?" can lead to information that

may provide insights on the symbolic interactionism that Denzin

(1989) identified as critical to an individual's meaning

construction within the personal and social experience. This tacit knowledge (Polanyi, 1958) can then lead the researcher to an enriched understanding of the phenomenon that, in the present case, may be of benefit to the larger SIE community. While centrally concerned with cognition, IPA allows the researcher to interpret what the participant discloses while recognizing that the participant is a complicated cognitive being that may struggle to express what he or she is feeling and thinking or may have motivations to not self-disclose (Smith et al., 2009). In IPA, understanding is derived through developing different perspectives through dialogue and then by charting any similarities or commonalities (Smith, 2004, 2007). In the present study, a greater understanding of the experiences was derived by allowing those who have experienced the phenomenon of SIE describe their perceptions of the what, how, and why in the context of their situations.

Research Questions

The methodology in research is driven by the topic and nature of the research question to be explored (Husserl, 1970; Leedy & Ormrod, 2010; Neuman, 2006). The following research question was the central focus of the present study: What is the lived experience and meaning attached to the experience of sociocultural adjustment of a native Western SIE while employed in the Near East? Responses to this research question also informed two related questions: How do SIEs employed in the Near East experience sociocultural adjustment in terms of their work, their interaction with members of the host culture, and in adjusting to the general living conditions and cultural practices of the new host culture; and how do SIEs employed in the Near East attach meaning to their sociocultural adjustment?

IPA provides the venue for exploring the meaning individuals ascribe to their experiences through a qualitative analysis approach (Smith et al., 2009; Smith, Jarman, & Osborn, 1999). IPA allows for using study participants as experts as their viewpoints originate from the center of the phenomenon (Sakala, Gyte, Henderson, Neilson, & Horey, 2001). According to Finlay and Gough (2008), the expert (participant) grants the researcher access into the participant's inner world. This allows the researcher to determine the meanings participants ascribe to experiences, which can only occur through an interpretative process.

Little is known about SIEs as the established body of research has been developed by studying traditional OEs and has relied heavily on organizational perspectives and definitions of adjustment (Biemann & Andresen, 2010; Bonache et al., 2007; Bruggeman, 2010). As the growing population of SIEs becomes more important in the international business community, a reasonable assumption is that SIEs can contribute to the transfer of knowledge regarding the phenomenon (Ratcliff, 2007). Through the current study of the meanings of SIE adaptation, contrasts may be found with those of the OE experience, thus leading to a deeper understanding of the SIE phenomenon.

Research Plan

SIEs currently working in the GCC region's education systems were used for the present study. Study participants were recruited through solicitation on various professional social media sites and through professional organizations and conferences related to the target population. Semistructured interviews were used for data collection. The interviews were recorded and transcribed verbatim. Analysis was conducted using IPA's hermeneutic foundation of inquiry and meaning— addressing the phenomenology of the participants' attempts to make sense of their own experiences and the researcher interpreting how the participants made sense of the phenomenon.

Study Participants

Study participants were selected using purposive sampling. Purposive sampling is an accepted nonrandom method of selecting participants (Cooper & Schindler, 2006; Creswell, 1998) that identifies participants capable of giving a specific and rich description of the phenomenon to be explored. Neuman (2006) stated that purposeful sampling is appropriate in a qualitative methodology as it allows for selecting unique cases that are uniquely informative as participants are members of a specialized population, which adds depth for in-depth study. For the present study, purposive sampling identified participants capable of giving unique and detail-rich accounts and experience of the phenomenon (Cooper & Schindler, 2006; Creswell, 2009; Neuman, 2006).

The present study's focus was on gaining insights on the perceptions of adjustment as experienced by SIEs working in the education sector. A respondent pool of prospective participants was amassed using individuals who were working in the GCC countries at the time of the study: Bahrain, Kuwait, Oman, Qatar, Saudi Arabia, and the UAE. Participants were SIEs from Western countries (Australia, Canada, Great Britain, Ireland, New Zealand, South Africa, and the United States) with a minimum 2 years of successful contract completion in the education profession and at the time of the study were employed by host organizations in the aforementioned Arab nations. All participants had to have expatriated on their own accord and were not relocated or asked to relocate by an employer. Participants were also restricted to those who could discuss their experiences, their meanings, and impacts experienced in English.

Recruitment was conducted through social media outlets that cater to GCC expatriate educators. Announcements were also made in training seminars and in forums and newsletters that service the sample population. I also invited participations through professional affiliations. Appendix A shows the solicitation letter. Prospective participants were prescreened using email exchanges, telephone calls, or face-to-face interviews. A sample size of 32 respondents was achieved.

Data Collection

The purpose of the present study was to gain insights into how participants experienced and made sense within the context of the phenomenon. IPA requires richness and depth, which can best be acquired through flexible, open-ended inquiry techniques such as focus groups, diaries, and interviews (Smith et al., 2009). I chose semistructured interviews as the most appropriate way to capture and explore participants' accounts and experiences.

Selected SIEs' experiences were explored mostly via semistructured, face-to-face interviews that were recorded and transcribed. In cases where face-to-face interviews were not possible, the following methods were used: web-based teleconferencing, phone interview, live chat, and email. IPA was employed to analyze individuals' responses.

Research has suggested that semistructured interviews may be the most effective approach for gaining insight and understanding of the experiences and feelings individuals associate with an experience (Fontana & Frey, 2003; Gillham, 2000; Yin, 2003). Kitzinger (1995) argued that the semistructured interview encourages participants to provide information that is "meaningful to them" (p. 299), which fosters more truthful and richer data. Smith et al. (2009) posited that semistructured interviews maintain an advantage of a guided conversation that allows participants latitude to share more in-depth information regarding their perspectives and gives researchers the flexibility for follow-up interpretive inquiry. Fontana and Frey (2003) stated that semistructured interviews allow researchers to explore seemingly contradictory data as well as gain more information regarding any gaps that develop in the data.

Recorded and transcribed semistructured interviews were used in the present study, (the interview protocol is described in Appendix B). Patterns were identified and discussed using statements from the various transcripts that describe the participants' experiences as well as provide insight and understanding of the participants' experience and feelings associated with the experience. The process was applied to each individual transcript. The original transcript was notated with exploratory comments as outlined in Smith et al. (2009). Smith et al.'s notation process concerning descriptive, linguistic, and conceptual comments was combined with the process of horizonalization of the data, viewing every statement or question as relevant or having equal value and meaning (Giorgi, 2008; Moustakas, 1994; Neuman, 2006). Areas of initial identification centered on statements that revealed the concepts of self, concept of place, personal identity, social identity, and the sensemaking process. It is acknowledged that the themes expressed changed and new patterns were identified. As the interviews were transcribed and patterns were discovered the coding was adapted

to recognize the emerging patterns.

Data Analysis

Qualitative methodology requires that data analysis

consists of classifying the elements of the phenomenon.

Moustakas (1994) described the van Kaam method of

phenomenological data analysis of complete transcription to

catalogue and describe the perceptions, experiences, essence, and

meaning of the experience. Patton (2002) stated that in a

phenomenological study the researcher "seeks to grasp and

elucidate the meaning, structure, and essence of lived experience

of a phenomenon for a person or group of people" (p. 482).

Transcribed interviews for each participant were read to

extract statements, phrases, and sentences that directly described

the participant's experience. Off-topic and verbal digressions

were edited, and sections belonging to similar topics were

grouped together as a unit of analysis as suggested by Neuman

(2006). Graneheim and Lundman (2004), Moustakas (1994), and

Neuman (2006) stated that grouping data into content areas is an effective method for detailed coding of units of analysis that allows for understanding the meaning a participant assigns to a specific account of a lived experience. The descriptions of the experience can be used to form meaning units or as Graneheim and Lundman (2004) termed "the constellation of words, sentences or paragraphs containing aspects related to each other through their content and context" (p. 106). The basis for all coding and theme identification became the meaning units. I developed a coding scheme for assigning labels to meaning units in keeping with Creswell (2009), Moustakas (1994), and Neuman (2006).

Data within each unit of analysis were reviewed several times, using constant comparison to refine themes, subthemes, and the coding scheme as needed. Zhang and Wildemuth (2009) emphasized that this process of constant comparison is critical in identifying new themes and in making differences in themes apparent. The process continued until the themes became saturated (Zhang & Wildemuth, 2009).

Trustworthiness

According to Hoyt and Bhati (2007), the strength of

qualitative research is the focus on "rich and complex

explorations of the experiences of a small number of individuals"

(p. 202) whereas quantitative methodologies often require

obtaining large, statistically representative samples. According

to Trochim (2006), qualitative researchers must be aware of

credibility, trustworthiness, reliability, and validation of the data

by being vigilante against potential threats to the validity of

phenomenological research. Cooper and Schindler (2006) and

Creswell (2007) listed the most common threats as inadequate

interviewing procedures, coding errors, incorrect transcription,

mistaken descriptions, unsuitable participants, and researcher

bias. In the present study, data reliability was protected using

procedures for checking and rechecking the data throughout the

study.

I acknowledge that semistructured interviews

encompassing open-ended questions regarding perception of an

experience had positive impact on the study's internal validity.

Bryman (2008) stated that the relationship between the variables studied and the participants' self-perceived efficiency will result in a very high confidence in the research's internal validity. Trochim (2006) stated that because the participants have the unique point of view that leads to a very unique ability to describe the phenomenon, participants can be deemed the most qualified to legitimately judge the credibility of the results.

Transferability, or external validity, the degree to which one can generalize to a larger population, was a small concern as the present study specifically related to the experiences of SIEs living in the GCC. Generalizability is only applicable if a similar study is conducted using a similar population with similar characteristics. Therefore, the representational value of findings is acknowledged as limited. While the external validity remains low, study findings can lead to future study concerned with expatriates' experiences and issues.

Finally, I employed the concept of *epoché*, the setting aside of any judgments, preconceptions, biases, and assumptions about the topic (Moustakas, 1994). As the method of employ, I maintained a reflective research journal as outlined by Lincoln and Gupta (1985). This journal consisted of three areas of reflection: daily schedule and logistics, methods and rationale, and analogous reflections. The daily schedule and logistics and methodology sections helped maintain consistency and uniformity in the research process. This attention to detail helped ensure that the participants' accounts were themed and coded as the participants intended as well as ensure that any theoretical assumptions had been developed based on theoretical models noted in the literature review. This also allowed for evaluating the research method's effectiveness and allowed credibility checks regarding the categories or themes that had evolved from the data. It also provided a review for discrepancies or errors in the data. The journal was also used as a form of triangulation, comparing two or more varied perspectives in the data.

In addition, I emphasized careful records management of all taped interviews, notes from interviews, and electronic copies of transcripts to enhance dependability. The analogous reflections were instrumental in my making clear my own personal bias, assumptions, and theoretical orientations through

recording my personal thoughts, feelings, reactions, frustrations,

and questions during the research process. This process is what

Lincoln and Guba (1985) termed "progressive subjectivity" (p.

28). Being aware of these attitudes, values, interests, and

assumptions helps researchers establish and maintain a level of

neutrality within the study.

Ethical Concerns

The study involved conducting face-to-face interviews or

interviews via electronic media, phone, or email. Prior to

conducting interviews, approval was obtained from the

University of the Rockies Institutional Review Board.

Individuals interested in participating in the study had confirmed

their interest though email to me. All participants received an

informed consent through email describing the research study,

the purpose of the study, participant involvement, and participant

consent. Signed informed consents (see Appendix C) were

collected during the in-person interview. When an in-person

interview was not possible, verbal consent was obtained and a signed copy of the informed consent was scanned and sent via email while the original was collected through one of the available mail courier services operating in the region. Informed consent is a key element in informing participants what they need to do and of any risks or benefits related to taking part in the study and is a requirement when any research involving human subjects is undertaken (Cooper & Schindler, 2006; Creswell, 2009; Neuman, 2006).

The consent form provided space for participants to sign and give permission for study participation and informed participants that all results would be confidential and that participants' identities would remain anonymous. The consent form contained the following elements: (a) study purpose, (b) voluntary nature of the study, (c) withdrawal procedures, (d) any foreseeable risks and benefits, (e) confidentiality process, and (f) my contact information. By signing an informed consent, individuals were stating their understanding and agreement to participate in the study. All participants received a copy of the signed form when they were given their interview transcript for verification. This was sent via electronic media when possible or mail courier service as per the participant's preference.

Before each interview, I reviewed instructions and the confidentiality statement to the participant word for word. Participants were advised that I would retain and secure information they provided for 3 years. At the end of the 3-year period all data will be destroyed in the most appropriate manner available at that time. All participants were advised on how they may withdraw from participation at any time without negative consequences. Participants could withdraw verbally at any time before, during, or after the interview or through email communication. Upon receiving a withdrawal request an official confirmation email would be sent to the participant confirming the request and informing the participant that all paper information would be shredded and that all audio recordings from the in-depth interview as well as all electronic transcription of the interview would be destroyed. No participants exercised the withdrawal option.

Confidentiality

All participant identification and any information learned about the participant are held in the strictest of confidence and will remain anonymous (Salkind, 2008; W. Walker, 2007). Participants were advised that results may be published, but no personal information would be provided and only I would have access to the data. Each participant was informed that I would transcribe the interview and that I would sign a nondisclosure statement ensuring confidentiality of participant data and participants' anonymity. To ensure confidentiality, I coded each interview transcript and subsequent study field notes to preserve participants' privacy. The code consisted of an alphanumeric system composed of the first and last letter of the participant's surname followed by a three-digit number. The list of participants' names and numbers will remain in a sealed envelope in a safety deposit box separate from the list of participant numbers and study data.

Summary

Since there is little literature concerning SIEs and their effectiveness during international jobs and lives, this research can be characterized as exploratory, inductive, and interpretative. A description of IPA research methodology and its foundation of a double hermeneutic accounting for both the participant and the researcher established the rationale of IPA as the phenomenological research methodology selected for the study. The nature of the research question aligned with purposeful selection as a preferred method of selection to meet the goal of examining a complex phenomenon, giving the rationale for the study participant criteria, sampling method, data collection method, reliability and validation process of phenomenological research, and the data analysis process. The discussion also supported the suitability of using face-to-face semistructured interviewing techniques to collect data.

CHAPTER IV: RESULTS

The objective of this chapter is to present the analysis

results from the data collected via the semistructured in-depth

interviews. IPA was applied to examine the participating

individuals' sensemaking of lived experiences. The coding of

specific elements of the shared experience (phenomenon)

provided the opportunity for interpreting the context of those who

have experienced the phenomenon of SIE to describe the

perceptions of the what, how and why as applied to the central

research question: What is the lived experience and meaning

attached to the experience of sociocultural adjustment of a native

Western SIE while employed in the Near East, as well as two

related questions: How do SIEs employed in the Near East

experience sociocultural adjustment in terms of their work, their

interaction with members of the host culture, and in adjusting to

the general living conditions and cultural practices of the new

host culture; and how do SIEs employed in the Near East attach

meaning to their sociocultural adjustment?

The results indicated that the SIEs' perceptions can be defined as nine self-identifiers that are related to the motivations for choosing the SIE path. The following perceptions or self-identifiers emerged from the interviews: an epic of discovery and not a career move, a life adventure, a romantic quest, a world explorer and traveler, a boundaryless careerist, becoming an international citizen, an avenue of escape, an altruistic hero, and the role of a lifelong learner.

Participants

For this study, 32 SIE educators working in the GCC were interviewed to obtain perceptions of their adjustment to their new organizational and social environment. The respondents were employees from government and private education institutions throughout various parts of the GCC. Originally, a purposeful sample size of 15 to 20 participants was sought. While Smith (2009) contended that for IPA a small sample can adequately provide a basis for a deep analysis, I agreed with other researchers that a sample size of a minimum of 15 and a maximum of 50 was acceptable (Bertaux, 1981;

Creswell, 1998; Guest, Bunce, & Johnson, 2006). Glaser and

Strauss (1967) discussed the concept of saturation, a point at

which the data offer no new information or explanation to the

process of analysis. At 32 interviews, I believed that the data

were not providing any new information or insights into the

emerging framework established by the earlier coded interviews.

At this point, I determined that saturation had occurred as

outlined by previous research (Crouch & McKenzie, 2006;

Glaser & Strauss, 1967; Ritchie, Lewis & Elam, 2003).

Participants were recruited through word of mouth and

social media, and all showed a high motivation and willingness to

participate in the study. Anonymity was maintained by giving

each participant an identifying marker to allow for tracking and

recording demographic data. To ensure confidentiality, if any

comments participants made could potentially identify them, I

replaced key words with the term ANON EDIT and redacted as

few words as possible to maintain the essence of the meaning in

the comment.

Regarding participant sociodemographics, the sample was gender balanced with 16 male participants and 16 female participants (this was not planned). The majority age range was 30–40 years (14 participants), 20–30 years (seven participants), 40–50 years (six participants), and 50–60 years (five participants). The number of years of experience as educators ranged from 3–34. The participants' experience as SIEs in the region ranged from 3–16 years. Only three participants had acquired some previous experience working abroad outside of the region, with the rest of the participants reported the region as their first expatriate experience. Participants' countries of origin are reported as follows: 11 from the USA, seven from the United Kingdom (one Scotland report included), five from Canada, three from Australia, and two each from Ireland, New Zealand and South Africa. Fifteen of the participants were married (including two married but spouses remained in home country) and 16 participants report as being single. Only four of the married participants had children living with them. None of the single participants reported having children living with them. Eighteen participations reported having obtained a bachelor's degree, 13

had a master's degree, and one had a doctoral degree.

Data Collection

Eighteen interviews were conducted in person. Because

of travel visa restrictions, all Saudi Arabia interviews were

conducted via Skype. In addition, travel and scheduling conflicts

resulted in the five Kuwait interviews being conducted via Skype.

The interview guide (see Appendix B) contained three question

groups, including approximately 12 separate subquestions,

addressing overall sociocultural comfort level related to the new

environment and exploring the subcategories of work comfort

level regarding new job responsibilities and new work

environments, general comfort level regarding living conditions

and the new host's cultural practices, and comfort level regarding

communicating and interacting with members of the host culture.

Not all questions were asked of all participants as the goal was to

cause participants to recall perceived critical-incident challenges

and their meaning to the participants' ability to adjust to the new environs. By getting the expatriates to tell their adjustment stories, clues to the meaning of their experiences were revealed.

All interviews were digitally recorded and transcribed verbatim. Skype interviews were recorded using VodBurner for Windows. I also made notes during the interviews to help clarify meaning to certain answers as an aid during analysis by providing help to explain certain answers and gain a deeper understanding through indicating strong emotional nonverbal cues and elevated tone and pitch changes in the participant's voice. Transcription took place directly after the individual interviews were completed. This allowed for a more effective application of notations and ensured the recognition and development of evolving concepts established during the analysis. This process also allowed for adaptations for future interviews. The transcription analysis took place concurrently with data collection from new interviews. All completed transcriptions were also made available to participants for verification if they so requested.

Interviews with Participant 1 and Participant 2 were
treated as pilot study interviews. These two interviews were
listened to and evaluated for analyzing interview structure,
question effectiveness, and my performance as interviewer. After
the transcription both participants were contacted and asked
follow-up questions to further clarify comments and details
provided. This process was then applied to the next six
interviews. By analyzing interview transcripts and reflecting
before more interviews were conducted, I could adapt the
question format for consequent interviews and ask more about
participant experiences. A major adaption to the process
determined after the first couple of interviews was that it was
important to transfer participants' demographic data to an Excel
spreadsheet so there were manageable data regarding the scope of
the participants and to allow for recruitment and scheduling of
participants to widen the participant pool and avoid a limited pool
from any particular geographic area.

Immediate interview transcription and using handwritten
notes allowed for effective development of the research journal

and also allowed for timely follow up with participants if clarification was needed. The transcriptions were completed in a chronological order, thus the lower the participant number (i.e., Participant 1, Participant 2, etc.), the earlier the interview was conducted.

Data Analysis and Results

After transcription was completed, an initial coding was conducted regarding examples of adjustment elements and strategies discussed in the literature review section. As the interviews and analysis progressed, coding was developed for emerging themes and patterns. New codes were added and previous interviews were reanalyzed for the presence of the identified themes. Table 1 lists the various coding used as themes and concepts were identified.

A second coding was conducted in which I recorded notations identifying observed areas that the participants commented on of the areas addressed in the research question regarding sociocultural adjustment in the work place, interaction with members of the host culture at work and in the community at large, and adjusting to the general living conditions and

cultural practices of the new host culture. The data were then

sorted and categorized as work adjustment, host culture

interaction, and living conditions/local practices.

Table 1 *Coding Key*

Theoretical domain	Marking code
Kohlberg social contract orientation	SCP
Kohlberg universal ethical principle	UEP
Value clarification	VC
Value adjustment	VA
Kincaid value convergence	KVC
Substitution	SUB
Janssens emotional adjustment	JEA
Schien underlying assumption	SUA
Navas domain politics & government	ND1
Navas domain work	ND2
Navas domain economic	ND3
Navas domain social relations	ND4
Navas domain family relations	ND5
Navas domain ideology: ways of thinking, principles, values	ND6A
Navas domain ideology: religious beliefs, customs	ND6B
Role clarity	RC
Job satisfaction	JS
Organizational commitment	OC
Psychological strain	PYSN
Communication competence	CC

Interpersonal competence	IP
Motivation and abilities	MA
Motivation choosing expatriate assignment	MEA
Self-pre-departure training	SPdt
Social support system	SSS
Formal mentoring	ForMen
Informal mentoring	InMen
Continual learning process	CLP
Sense making	SM
Personal identity	PI
Identity of others	IO

The initial coding goal was to identify participant references regarding adjustment in areas as defined by previous research discussed in Chapter II. But, as the interviews were reviewed and common themes came into focus, a secondary coding was developed and applied. These common themes became the focus of identification when examining the interviews.

The data collected revealed some common themes among the participants' responses. Many participants identified more than one of the themes as motivational factors present in their experience. The themes were defined as follows:

- the SIE experience as more an epic of discovery than a career move,

- the SIE experience as an adventure, to boldly go,

- the SIE on a romantic quest,

- the SIE explorer/world traveler,

- the SIE as a boundaryless careerist,

- the SIE as an international citizen,

- the SIE experience as an avenue of escape,

- the altruistic/hero SIE, and

- the SIE as a lifelong learner.

- While not classified as an archetype theme the role of serendipity, the experience not occurring by design of the participant, also was mentioned by the majority of the participants, so I recorded notations to look for any influence or effect it may play in the experience.

The SIE Experience Is More an Epic of Discovery Than a

Career Move

The concept of motivation is addressed when looking to attach meaning to the expatriate experience. The question of why the expatriate chose the move becomes the basis for attaching meaning to any definition of the experience. While all participants mentioned career and financial considerations as factors in why they chose to expatriate, the majority of participants, 27 of 32, reported that the decision centered more on a desire for a more personal experience of adventure, exploration, and self-discovery. Table 2 lists the most common participant responses.

Table 2

Participant Responses Regarding Reason for Expatriation Choice

Career considerations	*Personal considerations*
Financial incentive	Personal/family adventure
Lack of opportunity for advancement	Personal growth
Skill acquisition	Unique experience
Specialized job experience	Excitement
	Working in a different culture
	Being part of a meaningful change
	Finding self-fulfillment

138

Broadening mind/horizons

Enlarge personal comfort zone

Need a life change/in a rut

Explore travel

Curiosity about the region

Curiosity/ties to Islam

Family/ancestral ties to region

Motivation and expectation are crucial anchors in the process of defining and measuring any endeavor. The complexity of the SIE's experiences became apparent when the factors that created the essence of the SIE experience were classified and defined. The desire and impetus for SIEs to expatriate derived from a multitude of reasons and motivations. While not primarily driven by the career considerations previously discussed, a mixture of career and personal motivations measures the choice and the evaluation of success regarding the SIE experience. Motivation is a critical influence on anchors that affect the psychological process of sensemaking and adjustment. These two anchors have a strong influence in framing the evaluation and judgments of the experience's value.

The variety of reasons and motivations derived from the personal considerations participants reported were numerous but could be categorized into five general areas: adventure, international experience, escape/reinvention, altruism/heroism, and lifelong learning experience. It is important to note that none of the participants stated just one of these factors as motivations; in fact, the participants cited no less than three and in many cases all five areas as factors. A discussion of the individual categories and the relationship and influence of the career considerations within each follows.

The SIE Experience as an Adventure, to Boldly Go

All participants defined the experience as an adventure and excitement numerous times through the course of the interviews. Participant 2's comments typify the responses:

> I thought what an adventure, this will be exciting, quite an experience. Funny thing is I didn't even really know where the place was. I knew it was somewhere east of Europe near the Persian Gulf but again thought it will be an adventure.

Similarly, Participant 28 recalled, "I literally let the atlas fall open and dropped my finger on a country and said that's where I am going!"

While Participant 28 showed a higher level of dramatic flair in his response, both Participant 2 and Participant 28 demonstrated a desire for adventure. Five participants mentioned the impact on career as a primary motivational factor, but the majority mentioned career impact as a secondary concern. As Participant 15 stated, "This was about the experience, the job is just the way I pay for it." As the adventure motive was explored, a series of subthemes emerged.

The SIE on a Romantic Quest

In literature, the idea of the romantic quest is the opportunity to find the ideal or perfect world and life experience. A small number of participants described their experience as a quest that was filled with exciting events and interesting people who held the key for the participants to find their personal answers.

As Participant 19 said,

I still think it's an adventure, maybe I romanticize it a little too much, but I always think about the interesting people I meet, how this world is so completely different and foreign to what I knew and have experienced before. I can't but my finger on what I am looking for but I know there is still more to find.

The SIE as Explorer/World Traveler

The explorer maintains an irrepressible desire to travel and experience the unknown. The explorer is driven by the desire to see, learn, and experience that which is different from home. Participant 21 explained,

Once you start to travel, you have the opportunity to open your mind; there is so much to see to touch, to taste. Living here puts all that in reach; I can see the world one weekend at a time.

The explorer may develop a particular interest in a particular region or culture and seek to focus on experiencing all it has to be discovered. Participant 1 stated:

I have always been interested in this part of the world. All the ancient history and culture. Even more so since the Gulf Wars . . . When the opportunity to come see it and learn firsthand, I couldn't miss that.

There is also the desire to reconnect to a heritage or to come closer to one's religion. As Participant 16 put it,

> I am of Arab descent and a Muslim; this was the perfect
> opportunity to experience "my heritage" in its original
> form. I was curious what it would feel like to be in the
> "homeland." What I might be missing living here as
> opposed to there, in it.

The desire to experience new and different places, people, and

cultures or the need to connect to one's roots provided a strong

impetus to accept an SIE position.

The SIE as a Boundaryless Careerist

While the desire for adventure and excitement may be

primary in the motivation to become an SIE, career aspirations

cannot be disregarded. A number of participants mentioned the

motive of maximizing the opportunity to make and save money

as well as the possibility of advantageous status and benefits by

enriching their career through acquiring new skillsets and

competencies. Participant 9 explained,

> From a career perspective, I came to the Middle East to
> develop Arab language skills and network to help me with
> my planned PhD. Arabic is becoming a high-demand
> skill at home. I figured I would graduate, be able to read
> and write Arabic, which would lead to some amazing
> opportunities.

Financial incentives were sometimes mentioned as a factor in the decision. As Participant 22 stated, "The ability to take advantage of the free housing, no tax, and lower petrol and foodstuff costs compared to home was a significant factor in my choice." While the data suggested that career factors might not be a primary driver in the motivation to become an SIE, they appeared to be significant factors realized through becoming an SIE. Career considerations played a role as a factor influencing the decision to become an SIE.

None of the participants reported that the decision to become an SIE was part of any defined career track or life goal. Instead, it was more an occurrence of *serendipity*, a valuable and/or delightful discovery that an individual is not seeking at the time. Twenty-three participants reported that they were not actively pursuing the opportunity to become a SIE but that it was more a "right time, right place, chance of a lifetime" that coincided with a life stage circumstance they were experiencing at the time. Five participants reported that the employment opportunity was a coincidental reason for the relocation to the new country, meaning they were not seeking employment when

the opportunity presented itself. Twenty-nine participants had no

prior international work experience before accepting their SIE

position. Clearly defined goals and matrix of measurement did

not seem to be a high area of concern for the majority of

participants. Many participants stated broadly defined goals with

even broader definitions of how these goals were to be measured

as fulfilled or successful. The statement by Participant 31 is a

fair representation of the common response. When asked about

any defined goals or any deadlines set, this participant stated

> Naw, I mean I want to make some money, eliminate some
> of my debt, and maybe learn some more Arabic, travel a
> bit more. As far as a timeline, nope, haven't really got
> one. Taking it one year at a time.

When queried on goals or future plans, the SIEs indicated some

minor goals such as language acquisition, future travel

destinations, and some financial goals. When asked about

repatriation plans or length of stay intentions, six participants

could give a definite time frame with some specific goals to

accomplish but 23 participants gave a "We see how it goes" or "I haven't really thought about it" response, indicating they had no set plan. Participant 1 said, "If I don't put any concrete expectations on it then I can't get disappointed by it," indicating a "for now" mindset.

The concept of an adventure was presented as a somewhat nebulous destination based more on the individual's perceptions and feelings than within the overarching idea of a journey. Participant 22 demonstrated the general broadness of how the experience was structured regarding a focus:

> For me, I mean my big decision was about the personal adventure, you know, a journey. It was decision time for my life on which path to take, I decided to search for something new, not sure if I have found it yet. Guess I will know when I get there.

None of the participants referenced any career development plan or objective when recounting their experiences. They all referred to opportunities and challenges being spontaneous and out of their sphere of control and the focus on personal adaptability and resiliency as goals of attainment.

The SIE as an International Citizen

While closely related to the concept of adventure, 17 participants mentioned gaining the experience of becoming an international citizen as a factor in the decision-making process. This warranted inclusion as a separate entity. The international citizen mindset operates on a global level. Individuals with this mindset look to give and share ideas as well as get new expertise and insights. Participant 19 said, "Once you start to travel, if you have the opportunity to study abroad, you learn about different cultures [pause] understand that you've more in common than different. It allows you to change." All four participants with children cited this experience, which also relates to family influences in the process. SIE spouses, (including extended family) play an important role in SIEs' decisions to expatriate. Lifestyle factors such as social life and general happiness as well as opportunities for growth for the family individuals and family unit were also key elements. Participants with children cited educational opportunities for their children beyond the typical academic norms as major influencers in the decision process.

147

There is a belief that a physical encounter with foreign peoples and cultures has a much more powerful and meaningful effect for developing cultural diversity. Participant 15 stated,

> From a social perspective I wanted my children to be exposed to as many different cultures and languages as possible. It was important that they not be so ethnocentric to believe there is only one acceptable set of norms in the world. It was important that they learn to appreciate the beauty of different values across cultures, that they are a small part of a very large global community.

Additionally, the decision to expatriate to explore global work opportunities is given a degree of legitimacy when the SIEs' family members' international experience can be viewed as providing the same competitive advantage and offering the opportunity for growth and change that the SIEs themselves are experiencing. Participant 4 stated,

> The experience of living abroad for us in terms of myself and my family, I mean the education of studying abroad . . . It's expensive, and this way my kids are seeing the world from a nontourist point of view, which will give them life-changing experiences.

Multicultural was a descriptor participants often used. This descriptor was regarded as a moderate influencer in the decision to expatriate. The idea of integrating components of several different cultures was deemed important to gaining tolerance and understanding. While classified as a personal growth element it also blended with the career consideration as it was referred to in light of a career enhancement as well as a personal advantage. Participant 31 said,

> I studied three weeks abroad in high school and have never lost my amazement of living abroad. I had grown personally from it. When I married and had kids I wished for them to experience my experience, taste the deliciousness of interacting with different people, experiencing new things, becoming a better person, stronger with a brighter future.

The SIE Experience as an Avenue of Escape

The idea of escape is the drive to leave behind some aspect of the individual's life that is unfulfilling, painful, personally unsatisfying, or a source of conflict. The decision to become an SIE could be influenced by a single reason or a cluster of reasons. The factors participants reported were as follows:

- economic instability,

- lifestyle change,

- personal loss,

- lack of challenge,

- conflict with family,

- career transition,

- *wanderlust*,

- loss of belief in system,

- perceived lifestyle in new country,

- desire to control present/future, and

- conflict with supervisor/coworkers.

All 32 participants reported concerns regarding economic stability and made some reference to the 2008 economic downturn. Concerns regarding stability or opportunity for future economic stability were mentioned as factors in the decision to become an SIE. The six participants with defined goals and timelines previously discussed also addressed these concerns. Other financial concerns participants specifically mentioned were loss of benefits, increases in insurance rates, increases in workloads and hours required, and increases in taxes.

Eighteen participants cited feelings of boredom with the routine they had developed in their daily lives. Participant 26 recounted, "I was ready for a change in scenery, a change in my

150

life; I felt I was stuck and the chance came up so I came here."

Participant 16's response also demonstrated this mindset:

> I felt that I was stuck in a rut in the U.K. . . . In all
> honesty the money and opportunity for advancement
> wasn't much better, but I believed it would make my life
> more interesting. I realized what an opportunity to
> broaden my horizons even further.

Participant 1 sought escape from a system he had belonged to his

entire professional life but had come to feel was unbearable,

unrealistic in its demands, and personally demoralizing. "It had

just stopped working, it was too much. No resources, unrealistic

expectations. If I hadn't left I was most likely going to quit

teaching and find something else to pay the bills."

Personal loss and emotional distress can also be a factor

in the desire to escape. Participant 13 described her state of mind

when making the decision to relocate:

> It was oh, my God. My husband is dead and I looked at
> my life and asked what I am doing with it. I looked back
> at the last 25 years and thought they are gone, I need more
> from the next 25.

Personal loss can also be coupled with conflict and a lifestyle

change as Participant 6 recounted:

151

> I think there has got to be some personal reason based more on the divorce. After divorce, difficult, difficult time, because of the divorce I had to find a job, I had to find a home; I had to find a new life.

These factors are all extrinsic in nature and could classify as push factors, elements that encourage movement away from the circumstance. But some escape factors are intrinsic in nature.

One element of the adventure-seeking driver is the concept of wanderlust, the constant strong need an individual may possess that requires satisfying a constant urge to travel and is about not making any firm commitment of intention or duration. Participant 27's comments illustrate this:

> For me boredom is a constant thing, I often joke my second job is applying for jobs! Even if I am happy at my current job I keep applying for jobs! It's like my hobby. Maybe it's more like an addiction when I see something interesting, I apply. I am not too worried about if they hire me because I may not take it, but I like to have my options and who knows when it's time to move on.

Participant 19's comments echoed this as well. "I don't have that sense of rootedness a sense of have sense of home like this is where I need to plant roots. The world is too interesting and my passport still has some empty pages." While these values are

152

intrinsic and stem from the individual's values, attitudes, and aspirations, they may not imply boredom with current vocational and geographical circumstances as much as the individual's intrinsic need and desire for change.

Eight participants cited a lack of autonomy and expressed a desire to control their present and future circumstances. It was unclear if this perception was specific to career circumstances or general life circumstances, but the participants felt their previous position did not allow them to control their life journey. The belief driving the decision was that the new location would allow the individual the ability to make course changes in this journey. As Participant 18 stated, "I was not going anywhere. My place was set in stone. No career advancement seemed possible. Personally, I don't think anyone was going to let me change. I wanted to change but they had defined me." For Participant 2 the loss was directly related to the direction and situation with his employer. "They wanted to make changes and head a direction that was absolutely of no interest to me. It irked me every time they talked about the exciting new direction we were heading. I was so disillusioned." Participant 1 shared similar concerns and

feelings about his vocational circumstance before his decision to

be an SIE:

> I was really concerned about the pop star education craze.
> The whole academic world in the U.S. was crazy for the
> flavor of the month and pushing towards performing on
> the test . . . [it was] turning into a control business, there
> was no space for me to find teaching excellence.

Participant 12 expressed discontentment over the way social

policies and political tones were causing a high level of

frustration and disengagement:

> I felt that I was constrained by policies and practices in
> the main institutions, my frustration grew as there lacked
> the opportunity to engage with leadership. I had a
> growing level of resentment and no practical way to
> express it, I had little say in the affairs that seem to be
> affecting my life.

The sense of loss was the participants' only psychological

concern, but it was not as severe as the loss of autonomy or the

perception of a loss of challenge or opportunity for growth and

development. Statements like "I wanted to teach something more

challenging" (Participant 22) and "I didn't want to keep doing the

same thing over and over" (Participant 15) expressed the need individuals have for challenge in their jobs. Concerns about

monotony, workload increase, and lack of pay increase were also

mentioned as contributing sources of dissatisfaction, as described

by Participant 9:

> I couldn't have stayed in English factory anymore. I
> became a mouse on a treadmill. I can remember doing
> eight courses, back-to-back, and thinking "I'm going to
> die if I do this much longer more students more hours, no
> more money." It was exhausting.

The use of the terms English factory and treadmill allude to

Participant 9's belief in a loss of identity as well as autonomy in

his environment.

A lack of recognition and professional respect was also

identified as an escape factor influencing the motivation and

decision to accept a SIE position. Every participant interviewed

cited feelings that their profession was under appreciated and in

many cases not respected at the appropriate professional level.

Although it may be argued that many other professionals may

have similar beliefs and attitudes about their vocations, these

sentiments may be a unique circumstance to this homogenous

sample of professional educators. Nevertheless, statements like

"us versus them," "We don't care, it's all about the money,"
"Teachers are overpaid," and "Teachers have all kinds of time
off" are indicative of the general sentiment of a lack of
acknowledgment and respect.

The Altruistic/Hero SIE

Altruists/heroes are driven by an innate need to help and
contribute to other individuals and society at large by affecting
change through action and behavior. These traits were common
in this sample as the group was composed of educators whose
professional goal is affecting change through the art of teaching.
All 32 participants cited an altruist motivation as a factor in the
decision-making process, and five specifically mentioned the
excitement of being involved in what they perceived as a
transformation of the host culture through the teaching process.
Sixteen participants mentioned the desire to contribute to society
in general through teaching with 11 citing previous thoughts of
someday teaching in developing or foreign countries. Participant
11 said,

> I have always had a passion for teaching even when my family tried to talk me out of it. My parents threatened to not pay for my schooling telling me how those who can do those who can't teach. The same old arguments, you'll never have money, you'll be one of those boring intellectuals no one can stand. It's not about the money; it's about the light in a child's eyes when they get it. That's priceless.

While the SIEs expressed their desire to share through teaching, this statement also indicates a contradiction or dilemma the participants experienced. All indicated a high altruistic motivation in their chosen career field, but it became apparent that the financial benefits highly influenced the decision for the chosen location they currently resided. It also appeared that altruistic motivation blended with escape factors and financial concerns as the opportunity was serendipitous and not planned. When asked "Why Saudi Arabia?" Participant 8 said,

> I had just finished my Ph.D. and had to start paying off the loans. The recession had brought a lot of budget cuts to my district so the extra cash gigs were gone. I was looking at a second part-time job to make ends meet. It's up to you to find way to develop your life into what you want it to be, that's what I spent my whole career doing. This kind of financial opportunity wasn't going to happen in my hometown so the money and the chance to part of a reform I decided to come to the Kingdom.

157

The blending of the altruistic and escape motive was even clearer in Participant 26's statement:

> I felt like I was doing something that didn't matter, I was now a bureaucrat, not helping students reach their potential, what really matters in this job. All I saw was the negative impact of any change that I was part of. The best part of being a teacher is teaching.

It also appears that preconceived beliefs concerning the chosen destination highly influenced the altruistic motivations for destination selection. There was a uniquely strong altruistic/hero motivation for Participant 6. She had a strong conviction and determination to help her chosen country in its reform and stated a clear mission of developing a "generation of leaders with 21st-century skillsets." She believed this was her "calling in the profession" and that this job opportunity allowed her the greatest opportunity to carry out her "mission." The following portion of Participant 6's remarks emphasize the influence this conviction in her motivation: "I see my students becoming leaders in very high position one day and changing the attitude and direction of the country. By changing them for the better I change the country for the better."

Specific characteristics ascribed to altruism mentioned by other participants were "increasing another's future welfare" (Participant 4), "benefiting their lifetime" (Participant 22), and "The sacrifice is worth the payout when they are successful" (Participant 29), further supporting the altruistic factors' influence as the participants were acting upon this innate desire to contribute and affect change in the lives of the students they teach and in turn affect a greater social change for the host country. It is clear that these influences and beliefs are what drew the participants to the education vocational track. These motivational factors had a strong influence on their decision-making processes, and as will be discussed later had a strong influence on the adjustment process. How these factors blend in with the next factor of lifelong learning will also be seen. Participant 16's response demonstrated the mindset:

> I felt that I was stuck in a rut in the U.K. . . . In all honesty
> the money and opportunity for advancement wasn't much
> better, but I believed it would make my life more
> interesting. I realized what an opportunity to broaden my
> horizons even further.

When asked, "So would you define your choice as a good career move?" Participant 16 responded,

> I would say it was more a the correct life move, I am learning and experiencing so much more than I ever could have . . . to me it's an adventure and I am simply allowing me to make the most of life.

Participant 16's statements indicated that the experience was loosely associated with a career path but was more driven by the perception that the choice was an opportunity for personal development based on wider goals related to personal identity development. Participant 16 believes this was a chance for experiencing self-fulfillment and exploration and offering the opportunity to contribute and make a difference in the world as this participant perceives it. This is a move toward self-actualization. The traditional incentives of financial benefits, travel, and more leisure time are also factors in defining the experience. The acknowledgement that the job choice was in fact not significantly different in financial or career gain for the participants, all indicated the minor role career influence wielded. It is also important to note that the desire to leave behind or

160

escape an undesired life situation as well as dissatisfaction in the home country (as indicated by the "stuck in a rut" comment) was also a factor many participants echoed as a strong influence in the decision to become an SIE.

The SIE as a Lifelong Learner

Participant 1 stated, "I become a better person when I'm going outside my comfort zone where I learn something new interacting with people of different customs, language, and traditions. That's how I grow, that's life." Several participants also indicated that their SIE experience significantly impacted their personal growth and mentioned areas of communication, interpersonal skills, increased confidence, tolerance, and patience. These findings of life experiences were primary influencing factors in the SIE experience. Previous research has attributed expatriate success or failure to the expatriates' adjustment to the host culture. Study participants all acknowledged an understanding and commitment to the growth process, which they linked to the concept of adjustment.

Participants reported the importance of being self-aware and self-analytical as part of the growth process. Participant 1 stated,

> No matter the reasons for making the move, the excitement and glamour of the new life will wear off and you realize you wake up with yourself every day. As much as you're learning about the people and customs of this new far off place, you better look at yourself and realize that you are going to have to let go of you to a degree and prepare for change to happen, and still find a way to hold on to what is organically you.

Finding ease with concerns about security and cultural appropriateness.

Regional geopolitical concerns were not a matter of concern regarding overall safety or security for the participants. A major concern that did present was an awareness of vulnerability and job security related to the consequences of unintentional insult and offense regarding religious and cultural sensibilities. Participants acknowledged underlying concerns regarding communication and relationships with management and the locals. Participants also stated that the power students held was a prevalent issue.

The infused mixture of Islam and culture, a lack of a

unified central source of background information, and world

economic factors were sources of underlying workplace stress.

Censorship created levels of uncertainty for classroom

preparation and practice. Participants all noted various learning

curves and having to determine acceptable methodologies and

materials to use. Lack of centralized opinions from the

employing organization made the issue more complex. Support

from fellow expats proved inadequate as these beliefs and

opinions were often based on rumor and innuendo. The majority

of participants felt they had developed a sensible and working

methodology for addressing this issue but still had the underlying

sense that they were one mistake from having their job

terminated and being deported. Participants said the adjustment

required a tremendous amount of study and research concerning

the attitudes, practices, and social norms in their specific

community. SIEs had to come to a level of acceptance and

lowered concern while continuing to acknowledge the concern as

real. As Participant 31 stated,

My first "oh shit" moment came when I tried to use an
ESL reader I had brought from home which included
pictures of people on the beach, couples dancing holding
hands, pictures of a breakfast with pork chop, and pictures
of farm animals which included pictures of pigs. My
students started yelling "haram, haram," and later that day
I found myself in the office of the manager being told I
needed to black out all the unacceptable pictures or not
use the book again. For the rest of that trimester it
seemed every time a student wanted to complain I was in
the manager's office being told what a mistake I had
made. There were times where I thought I was going to
be fired. To this day I still have not had any formal
training on what is acceptable and unacceptable, but I
educated myself on Islam and local norms help curtail the
manipulation of students. But I always have in the back
of my mind that I'm one statement, one picture, one
mistake away from being out of a job.

When asked how this changed this participant's experience,

Participant 31 replied,

It means a lot more work than that I have to prepare all
my own materials, it also sometimes creates some stress
about the job in that I am often asked prepare the students
to be able to perform 21st-century skills in a global
marketplace, yet many of the things they would encounter
in that marketplace are censored. So I have chosen to
focus on the English language and leave the rest alone.

The expectation that participants were responsible for the content

of materials used in the class, coupled with the lack of any

unifying or detailed instructions from management, demonstrates

the complexity of participants' stress regarding having to decide

for themselves what materials were suitable or unsuitable while

struggling to accomplish the defined and required work goals.

This underlying concern appeared to be perceived as one over

which SIEs had limited control. These SIEs have taken

deliberate actions and made conscious decisions on how to

address and limit this stressful concern. This decision also came

with a negative effect on the SIEs' professional identities, which

will be discussed in more detail in later sections. Accepting this

reality and the subsequent cognitive appraisal of the SIE's own

perception regarding the level of the threat the circumstance

presented and the resulting measures of action indicated a

conscious and self-directed personal change.

Study participants all relayed an awareness that while

they were for the most part comfortable in their current position

they were very mindful that their status could rapidly change.

This concern centered on two cultural perceptions: the caste system and status and the possibility of violating Islamic religious and cultural tenets. First, while Western professionals and educators hold a higher status than most other expats, they are still considered lower than any of the local populations. This is also expressed as a concern in dealing with host national coworkers and Arab expat coworkers. The politics of power and authority can lead to conflicts between professional and personal ethics and principles in the profession's practice. The second concern leads to a constant awareness of cultural tenets and practicing censorship in curriculum and communications in the work environment, factors that relate to negative aspects of professional identity and that will be discussed in more detail in later sections.

The experience of difficulties in communication and relationships with locals.

While participants defined their experiences as an adventure and an opportunity for self-growth, they placed a high value on coming to understand the host culture. The participants all indicated a high level of confidence in their ability to communicate and understand their clients but also indicated this as a level of concern and frustration in the current environment. Participants all indicated a high desire and frequent attempts to socialize with host nationals outside of work. Many participants recounted their difficulties and disappointments with these attempts. They reported that it was easier to befriend expat Arabs than host-country locals. All participants commented on the importance of building a support network and communication system at the workplace. Rapport and collegiality were stressed as important factors in the education profession. The importance of rapport with the clientele (students) was also mentioned as a critical element in workplace success. All participants addressed recognizing and being aware of sensitive cultural issues.

All study participants expressed that developing associations with host-country nationals was an asset for learning local customs and practices and locating and making use of needed resources and materials to develop the work environment. But, all also expressed a level of frustration or disappointment in developing these relationships. Two factors were suggested as influencing factors: first, the small numbers of host nationals actually working in the education sector (the majority of host nationals in the sector had managerial/supervisory positions, which limited the scope and nature of interactions), second, while host nationals displayed the characteristics of hospitality and acceptance to the SIEs, interactions were most often kept at a distance and at a cursory level with very little spillover into the social realm. Participants also reported that it was much more common to develop strong bonds with fellow expat colleagues who were Arab but who did not originate from the Gulf States. Participant 2 described the distance:

> I have learned that there is a distinct difference among the Arabs I work with. The Gulf Arabs or "white Arabs" [reference to their wearing traditional local dress called Kandoras] are much more reserved and distant than the Levant or North African Arabs. I have been invited to a couple of Emirati weddings but I felt more a showpiece than a friend. Yet my Syrian and Palestinian coworkers have had me and my wife to their homes for dinner and social events. At-work conversations with the locals are very superficial or work related, seldom am I asked about personal things, not that there are anything close to water cooler conversations here but there is a deeper level of personalization with the fellow expat Arab teachers.

Participant 18 discussed the difficulties and conflicts in trying to

build social relationships with host-country nationals and

perceptions and conclusions as to causal factors influencing the

development of relationships:

> Anyone in Abu Dhabi would tell you it's not easy to
> make friends with a UAE native, or "local," as they call
> themselves. One could live here for years without ever
> getting to know a local. Some reasons for this: The UAE
> has a history of foreigners coming here to work and leave
> without putting anything into the country and this must
> affect how locals view expats. There are so many expats
> and so few Emiratis—the ratio is approximately 82% to
> 18%. Sometimes I've been told that because I'm Western
> and because I'm not Muslim. However, I also feel
> fortunate that I *have* made friends with an Emirati
> woman. It's surprising how open these women are once
> they're comfortable and also once they are certain no men
> are around. That being said, it is difficult when we have
> social time, which is always at my flat, I have to make
> several accommodations when she comes, some say is
> very unfair to me, that maybe I was even compromising
> my own culture to appease these ladies' requirements.
> That maybe I am not truly being myself when I am with
> her. Perhaps that is why I have not been invited to her
> home, perhaps it is too much work or maybe it's just
> impossible for them to accommodate.

The SIE assuming a level of personal responsibility for

difficulties in developing and maintaining relationships with

locals was a common theme.

Difficulties in communication and relationships with management.

Relationships with supervisors were even more complex for study participants. In the GCC region honor and reputation play important roles. The concept of *wasta*, the Arabic term for the role of status, influence, social standing, and "connection power," is also a major influence. In the GCC culture, respect for those in a senior position is extremely important. A supervisor assumes the role of a father figure and wants to build a relationship with a subordinate, but the relationship is skewed very steeply toward the subordinate. Information is gained so the superior knows the subordinate, but the level of familiarity is not shared in the subordinate-supervisor relationship. The position must be treated with the utmost respect. Appearance is extremely valued and saving face is paramount. The power structure is viewed from the perspective that each person has a very distinct role within the organization, and maintaining that role helps to keep order. Supervisors will seek input from subordinates and discuss matters with several individuals, allowing time to

170

navigate and reach the decision. Any feedback, criticism, or

challenges to ideas and opinions must be made in private, in

carefully constructed context and with the utmost respect for the

supervisor. Superiors are final arbitrators, and decisions are final

and should not be questioned. Subordinates wait to be told what

to do. Risk-taking is limited to those in decision-making

positions. Participant 9 described his first experience dealing

with a problem:

> I was in a meeting with several members of the faculty
> and a problem of attendance was being addressed. The
> principal was going around the room asking for
> perceptions of the problem. In the U.K. when you're
> asked about a problem it is not uncommon to give
> feedback to your boss on their decisions or company
> policy, but that didn't fly well here. Luckily for me my
> interpreter made some edits for me and I was able to
> avoid offense and damaging the relationship.

Similarly, superiors do not like to publicly chastise subordinates

as doing so could cause the subordinates to lose dignity and

respect. But this also creates an issue for Western expatriates

who feel they are not being given critical feedback. Participant

27 recounted:

My boss is real keen about not wanting to upset others in order to push through a deadline. But he expects deadlines to be met. It seems the management is reactive event rather than proactive time driven. If you try to rush things, you might anger your boss, so patience and flexibility are oh so needed. Arab management is so less structured than in the West but the pressure and follow-up heats up as the deadline approaches. Another thing I have learned is there is a tendency to avoid issuing bad news, and they often give watered down, rose-coated acceptances, which often mean no or perhaps.

Participant 1 recounted how items take several meetings to accomplish and that redundancy and repetition are elements of the process:

It may take several meetings to accomplish what could be handled by a telephone call or email. In those meeting you will be asked to repeat information you have previously provided multiple times. I have found out that repeating the same information indicates you are telling the truth. Supervisors often repeatedly ask the same question to see if your information is consistent and sometimes the questions are used to have you change your delivery. Arabs are tough negotiators but you have to be careful in the use high-pressure tactics. The acceptance of change is minimal, and if change is accepted it will be with little to no enthusiasm.

The issue of power and authority in the educator's role was another major concern participants noted. From performing professional duties to the use of behavior management and classroom policies, there is a complexity and potential for

conflict that provided a level of uncertainty for the participants.

Participant 15 gave the following examples of her experiences

with her beliefs and principles being opposite of those of her

students and local society:

> I found that in dealing with discipline issues I had very
> little control. Even if the student had violated class rules,
> enforcement of consequences was not going to happen. It
> was a tough adjustment. I also had to deal with being a
> woman. When the father came in I had to learn a new
> way to behave. I found that if I wanted to have any kind
> of respect I had to limit my behavior. I could act like
> home. As much as I found it biased and demeaning, the
> standards here are very different. I had to accept that this
> is not my house so I had to accept the fact that I wasn't an
> equal. I could talk or respond like I could back home. It
> just wasn't accepted. In the end I learned that it was best
> to smile accept and try a new management approach with
> the student, I had heard stories of knocks on doors and
> escorts with plane tickets in hand for those who chose to
> take a moral stand.

Participant 15's statement that as a Westerner and as a female she

had to modify her behavior when dealing with parents, especially

the fathers, and did so even though she found it biased and

demeaning reflects the reconciliation of her personal values and

beliefs with those of her new environment. It also reflect her perception of the differences between the Western society and the

Gulf/Arab society and her ability to adapt and to some degree

accept these different standards as well as an awareness of

potential consequences for failure to adjust. Participant 15

recognized that what she wanted to say and believed was

acceptable to say was in conflict with what was acceptable to be

said in the host cultural situation, and she chose not to say it.

Learning to accept the students' power in the

teacher/student relationship.

Participant 16 talked about the risky situation of getting sacked

because of student dislike.

> The students got a petition on a fellow teacher, no real
> reasons just that they don't like her. She was in real
> danger of getting sacked. This place can be really unfair
> sometimes. . . . It only takes one student not liking you,
> being mad, it's always a risky situation, and it's almost
> never a real academic issue its just how they feel.

This passage underscores the underlying concern that

professional SIEs maintain in deference to the risk of losing their

job because students can exert power to remove them from their

position for no other reason than to be vindictive with teachers who have upset them. Participant 28 recounted how student's

words can create difficulty:

> I had disciplined a student and was called into the office
> by the principal. But instead of discussing the student's
> behavior I was confronted as to why I had braided hair
> and wore lipstick. (Participant 28 has a dreadlock
> hairstyle). You see, the student went and complained that
> I was corrupting him. That my hairstyle and his
> witnessing me applying Chapstick to my lips was
> feminine behavior and that I had no business telling him
> how to do anything. I ended up transferring to another
> school but I learned a valuable lesson about how to
> present myself in public, how little status I actually had in
> regards to the locals. I didn't cut my hair but started
> wearing the local headdress to cover my hair at school. I
> also refrained from using care products until I am quite
> sure I am alone in the classroom. I also handle discipline
> quite differently, making use of group pressures much
> more.

Participant 28 found that he had to compromise or modify his

behavior and appearance to avoid conflict. He was able to

modify or marginalize his own values to maintain his

environment. This illustrates the influence of wasta and the

potential threat of power in which students and parents can create

problems for SIEs. The allegation in Participant 28's case was

not investigated but simply accepted and then accepted again

when recounted. Again, a realization that the participants

acknowledged as part of their position's uncertainty and

precariousness.

The SIE Redefines Professional Identity

All study participants acknowledged the realization of

change related to their professional identity. But, participant

perceptions were split regarding whether this change was positive

or negative. A common theme for those who characterized the

perceived change in their professional identity as positive was the

excitement and adventure of overcoming the defined challenges

and conflicts and using them as opportunities for growth and

advancement on both professional and personal levels.

Participant 17 remarked,

> I understood that my role was to advise, support and
> mentor. In order to do this I had to learn as much as I
> taught. It was an opportunity to reevaluate the knowledge
> and skills and to grow and develop them further. I was
> well aware that I didn't have all the answers.

Participant 24 made the following comments regarding the

change experienced:

> I came into the classroom five weeks into the semester. I
> was thrown into the classroom with no guidance, no
> curriculum, no management plan save my own, and that

was an issue, the behavior management is a serious issue,
no class lists, no standard class schedule . . . Nada. Phew,
I would be lying if I said I didn't think about leaving, but
as I adapted, made friends with the Arab expats. Learned
about the kids, I created my own materials, unit plans, and
curriculum. I did my best and it worked sometimes,
sometimes it didn't, but I felt good about the experience.
I found confidence and was actually starting to enjoy the
challenge aspect of the situation. I actually think my
surviving that first year was the best year as teacher I
have had.

Participants who found the experienced affect changes positive

related them to their established values regarding the importance

and benefits of continual learning, self-fulfillment, and progress

toward a level of self-actualization. These attitudes demonstrated

an increase in professional self-image and demonstrated self-

growth.

The participants who defined the perceived challenges as

negative gave the following differentiations: a loss in

professional self-image, the inability to recognize and express

one's self, finding oneself in a stage of professional survival, and

a sense of failure. Participant 31 expressed the following

sentiments:

177

I found the experience the first year as horrible. I received no empowerment or appreciation from the administration, students, or parents. It was all directives, new requirements of non-teacher-related analysis, and no one in authority listens to your worries or needs. I was going to resign, but personally I can't imagine myself doing anything else as a job, to me teaching is as sacred of a profession as there is. I had to find other ways to get fulfillment and come to terms that teaching in the ANON EDIT was not making me a better teacher. I had to focus on other goals for coming as a source to maintain and handle the feelings"

I asked Participant 31, "How it affected your profession?

I mean, has it changed you as a teacher?" Participant 31

responded,

Since I have arrived here my teaching style and preparation have completely changed. Completely. I basically never work with published materials anymore; I wouldn't say I'm phobic but realistic in that while they make the job back home easier, here they just waste time. And I think that would apply to any professional development, I haven't taken a course or read a professional book because, quite frankly I just don't have any use for me here. And I also don't think I will be teaching when I decide to go home, or if they apart decide for me [said laughingly]. My skills have diminished and I don't want to work that hard when I get back home"

Participant 31's comment and demeanor highlight a seeming

contradiction in the adjustment and value process regarding his

identity as a professional educator. Yet his demeanor suggested he really did not want to go home and was comfortable with his

diminishing skills as a professional.

Participant 1 stated:

I have seen my teaching skills diminish as what I have
done for years back home does not apply here. Behavior
management and dealing with the administration, lesson
planning, grading, testing, all of it are going to be a major
adjustment for me when I return back home and try to
teach again. Honestly it is the financial goals I have that
drive my ability to maintain and stay in the job.

Whether the experience has been designated positive or negative,

what the data indicated is that SIEs are reflective practitioners in

developing a deeper understanding and making sense of their

situation and what affect the experience has had on their identity

as they define that identity.

Adjustment becomes part of the adventure.

Previous research regarding adjustment identified three

psychological needs that centered on the following subcategories:

communication and relationships with peers, identity and

satisfaction, and job security/financial incentive. The data

indicated that identity and satisfaction may be the most difficult

areas for the SIEs. The participants identified issues regarding job security, cultural appropriateness, and communication and personal identity as main factors in their adjustment process.

The continuous process of defining one's values.

The initial analysis revealed that all the SIEs viewed the experience as an opportunity for adventure. Most also discussed the need to evaluate and define their values and who they were and what they wanted. Participant 9 stated,

> My identity has and will always be Irish wherever I venture, that will never change, but there have been many aspects of the cultures I have experienced that I have adopted and really enjoy so I have made them a part of who I am.

Study participants recounted experiences and the level of deep analysis these experiences elicited for them. The SIEs acknowledged these reflective practices as contributing to the building of awareness and adjustment competencies in difficult and often frustrating environment as summarized by Participant 1:

> I don't necessarily share or even agree with some of the values here, but I can understand them in the historical and religious context. I mean I have so many new levels of tolerance I never knew I had, which has been so crucial to my being able to avoid a lot of anguish, stress, and

rejection that would have found me going home like so many others I have worked with.

Many participants further stated that the process is perhaps an end in itself; a cycle of lifelong learning that contributes to the individual's personal growth. Participant 2 stated,

> It's a beautiful process, the coming to an understanding of who I am and how I relate to all these around me, learning new social codes, beliefs, ways of life, and looking to see how they fit into my value system. I realize that I have synthesized many aspects into my own life.

While the pervasive thought seems to be it is best to "just keep your head down and drive on" in dealing with value conflicts, it would be inaccurate to say that all participants were accepting or comfortable with perceived injustices. Participant 12 said,

> I would say that I really get on with the Arab people here. I mean I haven't met an individual on a personal level that I didn't get on with. I like being here but at an institutional level this place can be and is often very frustrating. There is a bleeding lot of unfairness in the way the society is set up. The local folks are really favored and . . . um. Well, what makes it bleeding worse is they don't seem to appreciate it and how much the expat population has contributed to that favored status. The way they treat the labor force is demeaning. I make thirty to forty times what they make in salary, I mean they are the reason this place isn't still just a large sandbox and I bet my status as far as class is concerned is no higher than theirs in their home country. I often feel really

181

uncomfortable when they call me sir and bow to me. I feel I am placed way above my background. That being that, I am really disgusted in the lack of respect most of the locals show for these blokes. I mean I know there is no way that the world will elevate the cleaner to favorite status but come on is [it] not unrealistic to say add on a little respect, would it hurt? When I mention it to my Arab colleagues, especially the Emiratis, I am chastised and told that they are where they are supposed to be and Hamdu'allah they are happy to have what they have.

When asked how he deals with it, Participant 12 responded, "I remind myself that even in the West we have a hierarchy and we disparage certain professions and classes. Maybe they are more honest in that they are up front and open about it."

Participant 12 has found a rationalization to help balance his conflict with his personal value of treatment of others with his perceived value held in the Gulf region. While he at one level equated himself with the laborers in the region he postulated that perhaps there is no difference but that the local society is perhaps more open and honest in its treatment of the value. Participant 7 stated,

> It is such a servant society and they are so physically lazy. There is a lack of self-sufficiency and a privileged and pampered lifestyle. I mean they pull up to coffee shop or a small market honk their horn and some comes out and

serves them. The students here are the same way. It's always teacher help me help. Help with the exam, help me with the mark. What they want is for you to make it easier or to flat out give them the grade. It makes me at times just a glorified manservant. It seems to me that there is always a servant to do the job for them. They want to pay me to do their job I guess that's the job so okay I'll cry all the way to the bank.

Participant 7 showed an attitude of marginalization and justification as he made a generalization of the society as a whole and accepted the host culture's perceived attitude as not his responsibility and therefore not a conflict for himself. Participant 10 showed a similar ambivalence.

It's a two-sided coin working here. There is a level of respect afforded us having White faces, Western names, I'm called Madame whatever. Um. But at the same time there is always an undercurrent of yeah, right, you're not going to make that happen. I mean there is always the feel of I'm just a worker and I will be told what will happen. And support from up top, not going to happen, I feel completely disposable, completely replaceable. You have to be very careful to not complain, not correct, not suggest. If they don't like you won't be here.

This comment highlights the conflict and the marginalization of personal values to deal with the complexity of simultaneously feeling respected and feeling powerless.

The SIE Adjusts

Adjustment may best be described as a process of personal change concerning the individual's understanding, level of awareness, and interpretation of the events experienced. Cognitive shifts in self-concept and sense of belonging are influenced by the motivations for choosing the SIE experience. These cognitive shifts are the critical component in the SIE's sensemaking. The learning process allows the SIE to develop mental maps and a knowledge base by which to navigate the new host culture's nuances and norms. The ability to accurately interpret situations and chose appropriate behavioral responses was reflected in the participants' attitudinal expressions. The desire to seek personal growth allows for flexibility in sensemaking of perceptions regarding cultural challenges in conflict with personal values. This dynamic attitude of expectation and willingness to accept the role of these challenges also seems to be evident in this study's participants. The ability to adapt seems to be linked to elements of personality traits participants exhibited. Five common personality traits or dimensions are defined next using the Big Five Personality

Inventory's general descriptors.

Openness to experience.

As discussed in the previous section on motivation,

participants expressed a high degree of desire for adventure and a

high degree of intellectual curiosity regarding discovering

elements of the new host culture. The influence of serendipity

also indicated a high level of preference for variety and change as

well as a level of independence. Participants also indicated a

level of proactivity regarding their circumstances once the

decision was made. They reported decisions and actions that

denoted a level of creativity in approaching conflicts and

adaptations regarding their new environment. Participant 8 said,

> You hear experts and talking heads say get out of your
> comfort zone to grow, I think I have stretched that thing
> so far I don't have a comfort zone. I live in the no
> comfort zone, and I love it.

Conscientiousness.

In this area study participants showed a middle-of-the-

road behavior regarding the trait with a balance between being efficient/organized versus easy going/careless. Concerning

elements of their professional life, participants expressed a

tendency to be organized, exhibited **self-discipline,** and preferred

planned rather than spontaneous behavior. They expressed a

more "roll with the punches" attitude regarding their personal and

social lives and were willing to be much more spontaneous in

choices and decisions. Participant 23 stated,

> When it gets a little tough I just take a little time, have a little "hakuna matada" moment and make a plan. I remind myself that the next minute it all can and probably will change so why get upset. Besides the weekend's always coming and the airports are open 24/7.

Extraversion.

Participants expressed high levels of energy,

assertiveness, and sociability during the interview process. They

genuinely appeared to be enjoying the social process and sought

interaction with others in the environment, often exhibiting

talkativeness with others in the surrounding environment during

the in-person interviews. Participant 15 said,

> I can't express how proud I am of myself for taking this risk, from facing these things that seemed so hard and scary but now I wonder why I worried at all. I have

increased my self-confidence, I talk to strangers all the time, form relationships and have made new friends with folks from all around the globe.

Agreeableness.

Participants also expressed a high level of compassion and cooperation in their narratives. The indication of a high level of trust and belief in the innate goodness of others coupled with altruistic values of wanting to help and affect change in their new environment. Participant 12 said,

> It sometimes is still unbelievable that I live and work in another country. I am blessed with such a mind-expanding and a rewarding experience . . . I do not believe that I would be the person I am today if I had not come. I realize that a little contemplation is healthy for the soul and it helps me to remember that it's okay and it will all work out. If I can do this I can do anything. Live by example and maybe make the world a little better.

Emotional stability over neuroticism.

Participants did report incidences when they experienced levels of frustration and unpleasant emotions. However, situations that generated anxiety over discontentment were all reported as short lived and tempered with rational awareness and purposeful decisions designed to alleviate and deescalate the

187

situation. Participants reported high positive self-esteem and

proactive decision-making strategies that enhanced feelings of

autonomy and confidence in their abilities to adapt. Participant

29 said,

> Man . . . I really feel like I can handle anything life throws at me. This Middle East adventure, learning a new language, how to navigate and function in a new and different culture has been a vastly eye-opening experience to what I am truly capable of. I have never enjoyed learning so much in my life. I think I've grown more in the last six years than the previous thirty-two of my life.

Adjustment as an ongoing process.

The majority of participants also defined the adjustment

process as a cyclical effect nonspecific in nature and difficult to

identify. It was suggested that the adjustment process is never

completed but is more a constant process of realization and fine-

tuning to subtle nuances of living in the new environment. As

Participant 2 stated, "You have to go through the process several

times, mostly it is small things that add up, sometimes it's a big

thing that develops, but I am not willing to say that I am

completely over adjusting." When asked how this participant

would judge or rate the experience, Participant 2 said, "It's not easy. . . . I find a great sense of pride in that I have grown and learned along the way and the adventure is far from over." Participant 2's final statement denoted a common theme participants expressed that while the adjustment process is often difficult it also elicits a sense of value and accomplishment as phases are completed.

Adjustment requires humor and humility.

While the process is experienced with varying levels of intensity, all participants mentioned that a sense of humor and a level of humility to survive the adjustment process were needed. Humor was evident in the participants' attitudes and tones as they recounted their experiences. Both presented in descriptions of experiences and perceptions as demonstrated by Participant 3: "From igloos and sled dogs to sand dunes and camels, but so far I am really liking it." Humor was also often used in the form of self-deprecating humor as expressed by Participant 4: "Oh my God the food is to die for, that's why Kuwait is always on those lists of most fat people, sorry, but it also why I love the dress here. It hides my guilt."

Humility was also suggested as a necessary quality for adjustment. The experience of relocation to a new environment presents a challenge to SIEs when they are confronted with making sense and reconciliation preconceived notions of regions, cultures, values, and their self-perceptions. It can require a shift in self-definition. As Participant 24 stated:

> Starting over in a new strange place where I couldn't communicate with anyone. You have to let go of what you have known, let go of yourself, to let some change happen, yet you also have to still hold on to what is essentially you. With time you'll build a life, discovering more of yourself at some basic level are gaining in life experience.

The Need to Develop Resiliency

In some cases where professional identity levels were lost or unfulfilled, SIEs developed coping mechanisms to help bolster their resiliency. It appears that compromise and sensemaking bolster resiliency. These adjustments to perceived values and self-identifiers may have been accepted as necessary in the pursuit of more valued objectives that tied into the experience's primary definition as adventures or self-learning opportunities. They also could be simple compromises of values that may not have been held as deeply. Participants indicated that some loss in

one aspect of their self-definition can be replaced with increases

in experiences that increase other needs or expectations. In

essence, replacement or substitutions also seem to bolster

resiliency. The participants also displayed a level of awareness of

this process and developed means by which the substitution can

be accomplished. Using social networks and associations with

groups or activities that provided rejuvenating energy seemed to

be an important component of the overall adjustment and ability

to maintain the SIE status. Participant 16 commented,

> It's a trade-off, it's a trade-off, the drag and drain of work
> is heavily outweighed by the lifestyle opportunities, the
> beach, travel, cultural exploration, the people from all
> over the world, if I have to put up with six hours of
> drudgery, it's worth it. I mean, learning Arabic, how to
> play the lute, and the dune bashing, and five or six less
> hours from mostly historical places in the world and make
> good money so really working ain't that bad.

The need to develop connections to help fill voids or holes in

knowledge and support has been greatly enhanced by the advent

of social media. Participants identified social media as a method

they used to develop diverse connections and networks.

191

The Role of Social Media in Filling Holes

All participants recounted the role and significance of social media in all aspects of their adjustment. They credited the positive influence of the ability to stay connected with loved ones in other parts of the world in a real-time manner as a source of reinforcement and rejuvenation. Participants also stated that social media was very helpful and in some cases instrumental in developing support systems and gaining insight and information by allowing connections to a larger pool of expats sharing the same experiences, enabling a larger body of information to be shared much more quickly. Socializing afforded through social media helped SIEs find a sense of belonging and added opportunities for developing self-satisfaction. The role of social media in developing new friendships and gathering needed information regarding problems seem to support the strengthening of resiliency necessary for adjustment. Participant 7 said,

> Facebook, Skype and Google Talk were lifesavers. I was able to develop connections outside of my limited work opportunities, people who were in the same circumstances

and having those same problems that I was. It was a lifeline to find people who had the same interests as I did. Attending those functions and making new friends gave me the needed energy to survive things I felt at times without control.

Social networks appeared to have a support role in expat adjustment for SIEs through aiding in building relationships and support systems as well as being a source of information shared between those experiencing the same circumstances.

Conclusion

The purpose of this chapter was to present the analysis of the data collected from the participants. The data addressed the SIEs defining of the experience as one or more of the following nine archetypes: the experience is more an epic of discovery than a career move, the experience as an adventure, a romantic quest, the chance to act as an explorer/world traveler, a boundaryless careerist, becoming an international citizen, an avenue of escape, the opportunity to act as the altruistic/hero, and fulfilling the role of a lifelong learner. Taken in total leading to an opportunity for self-growth and learning.

The data demonstrate a perception of growth in areas of communication, tolerance, patience, increased self-confidence, and fulfillment towards self-actualization. Comments on adjustment in the workplace detailed conflicts within the area of professional identification mostly showing a negative perception of the outcomes but not enough of a negativity to taint the experience as a whole. The work environment's circumstances and reality were a major source of stress and conflict for the SIEs. While all practical adjustments were made, the underlying stress and concern regarding job stability remained a conscious issue for the SIEs. Also, interaction with host-country nationals also seemed to be a difficult resolution. General life adjustment seemed to score the highest in overall adjustment experiences. A recognized awareness of the need to compromise and substitute lead to opportunities to fulfill the experience defined as an adventure self-growth opportunity. The intentional use of social media and other directed activities seem to be a method for bolstering resiliency and allowing for sensemaking and adjustment.

CHAPTER V: DISCUSSION

The purpose of this chapter is to take the study findings and discuss them in connection with the study's theoretical framework and stated purpose to explore and examine the meaning and experience of sociocultural adjustment of a native Western SIE while being employed in the Near East. In addition, I explore the meaning attached to the sociocultural adjustment in terms of SIEs' work, their interaction with members of the host culture, and in adjusting to the general living conditions and cultural practices of the new host culture as well as how SIEs employed in the Near East attach meaning and understanding in forming their perceptions of their personal sociocultural adjustment.

The education sector has experienced a recent upswing regarding the SIE phenomenon, especially in the GCC's economically emerging countries. The GCC has invested a very large portion of its resources into the globalization of education with a high emphasis on the development of 21st-century skills and using English as the language of international business and science. This focus has led to the influx of SIEs from the Western countries of Australia, Canada, Great Britain, New Zealand, South Africa, and the United States. This emergence of SIEs, individuals who search out and undertake employment outside of their home country, has not been studied in detail. Much research has been conducted on the factors that contribute to expatriate failure and possible remedies to counteract these factors, yet the turnover rates are still estimated at 70% to 90% in the GCC region (Al-Bawaba, 2012; Al-Waqfi, 2012). These rates have a significant financial impact for the GCC economy as expatriate employees are estimated to be 58% to 89% of the total workforce in the GCC countries that significantly rely on these employees (Al-Bawaba, 2012; Al-Waqfi, 2012). The SIE's economic impact is also significant as the SIE most often incurs relocation costs, and failing to complete the agreed-upon contract results in the hiring organization seeking recovery of pay and incentives provided during the tenure (International Labour Organization, 2013).

I sought to examine the experiences of SIEs who have

successfully completed a minimum of one contract term (2 years)

in the education profession in the GCC to identify and understand

the levels of adjustment and retention success as defined and

experienced by these successful individuals. I also sought to

provide possible insights that may help both SIEs and

organizations in the management, strategies, and methodologies

that provide opportunities for success. The following research

question was the central focus of the present study: What is the

lived experience and meaning attached to the experience of

sociocultural adjustment of a native Western SIE while employed

in the Near East? Responses to this research question also

informed two related questions: How do SIEs employed in the

Near East experience sociocultural adjustment in terms of their

work, their interaction with members of the host culture, and in

adjusting to the general living conditions and cultural practices of

the new host culture, and how do SIEs employed in the Near East

attach meaning to their sociocultural adjustment? The chapter

will present a general interpretation of the findings, present a concept for a model of adjustment, discuss implications for

current theory and suggest implications for future practice

Interpretation of Findings

My intention for conducting the present study was not to

generate knowledge that could be generalized to other SIE

populations. I sought to interpret the experiences reported by a

group of Western professional educators working as SIEs in the

GCC region.

Influence of Personality

Data from the present study support previous research

findings that personality may be important antecedents to the

adjustment process and specific personality elements may

influence both the SIE's motivation and resiliency (Ang, Van

Dyne, & Koh, 2006; Caligiuri, 2000b; Swagler & Jome, 2005).

This ability of adaptation seems to be linked to elements of

personality traits participants exhibited. Five common

personality traits or dimensions were defined using the general

descriptors of the Big Five Personality Inventory (John, Donahue,

& Kentle, 1991) and were identified as commonly exhibited by the participants. The five common traits and specific qualities identified are listed in Table 3.

Prior research has suggested that personality may have a major role in an individual's adjustment process (Ang et al., 2006; Caligiuri, 2000b; Deci & Ryan, 2002; Swagler & Jome, 2005; Ward et al., 2001). Deci and Ryan (2002) determined that individuals with a high sense of self-determination and a strong desire to learn, when confronted with an unresolved conflict, chose to perceive the unresolved conflict as a new learning goal to be acquired. Ang et al. (2006) reported that individuals with high degrees of autonomy, competence, and relatedness viewed the challenges presented during the adjustment cycle as the opportunity to enhance their conscious awareness and set a personal goal to resolve the conflict. Mendenhall and Oddou (1985) found that individuals who experienced high levels of adjustment had a very high belief in themselves and their ability to effectively make sense and resolve any conflict. Participants in the present study gave the same general sense of high self-efficacy as they discussed their experiences and adjustment

conflicts.

Table 3

Big Five Personality Inventory Common Traits and Specific Qualities

Common traits	Specific qualities
Openness to experience	Ideas (curious)
	Fantasy (imaginative)
	Aesthetics (artistic)
	Actions (wide interests)
	Values (flexible/under constant evaluation)
Conscientiousness	Competence (efficient)
	Order (organized)
	Dutifulness (not careless)
	Achievement striving (thorough) *not specific to career
	Self-discipline (not lazy)
Extraversion	Gregariousness (sociable)
	Activity (energetic)
	Excitement-seeking (adventurous)
	Positive emotions (enthusiastic)
	Warmth (outgoing)
Agreeableness	Trust (forgiving)
	Straightforwardness (not demanding)
	Altruism (warm)
	Compliance (not stubborn)
	Modesty (not show-off)
	Tender-mindedness (sympathetic)
Emotional stability	Lack of anxiety (tense)
	Very low levels sporadic depression (not contented)

Self-consciousness (shy)

Low levels of vulnerability (not self-confident)

Note. Adapted from "The Big-Five Trait Taxonomy: History, Measurement, and Theoretical Perspectives, by O.P. John and S. Srivastava, 1999. In L. A. Pervin and O. P. John (Eds.), *Handbook of Personality: Theory and Research* (Vol. 2, pp. 102–138). Copyright 1999 by Guilford.

The SIE Experience is More an Epic of Discovery Than a Career Move

The data collected indicated that when the SIEs attached meaning to their experiences, motivation for the relocation seemed a major influence in the sensemaking and adjustment process. The following five of the nine thematic metaphors best describe the associative motivations that influenced the decision to become an SIE:

- the SIE as an adventurer/explorer,

- the SIE as an international citizen,

- the SIE as an escapee,

- the SIE as an altruistic hero, and

- the SIE as a lifelong learner.

While some motivations may be stronger in certain individuals, it appears that most participants displayed a blend of these motivations wherein they were related and often feed into each other was as the source of motivation.

Another evident component of motivation was the role of serendipity in the decision to become an SIE. None of the participants stated that becoming a SIE was a career or personal goal. Some expressed the dream or fantasy of such an experience, and all mentioned that the opportunity was one of chance or timing and not a strove after endeavor. This happenstance was further demonstrated by the participants expression a general "for now" attitude concerning intentions and continuation planning of the experience.

The values of lifelong learning and self-growth coupled with the ideal of becoming a world citizen also seemed to have a heavy influence in the sample. Of the motivations, it can be implied that this desire for growth was a resiliency factor as it allowed the individuals an open-minded perspective in confronting challenges and conflicts. The blending of motivations coupled with the often-cited role of serendipity was

most directly tied with the SIE as an escapee. Yet another duality

is that in this context the external factors that cause discontent in

the home country were seen more as opportunities than obstacles

in the new environment. This may be due to the lack of

perceived permanence of the situation because of the increased

belief in the individual SIE's autonomy and control in relocating

again. Another contributing factor was the classification of these

obstacles as learning adventures. The attitude presented was one

of these challenges being positive in nature.

The motivation of the move is directly tied to what

Magnini and Honeycutt (2003) defined as a *learning orientation*.

Learning orientation refers to individuals' ability to adapt by

using and modifying their own competence and skill levels and

mastering new skills in new situations. It highly involves the

individual's desire to learn from his or her experience, to seek

new and challenging experiences, and to have the opportunity to

gain skills and feedback to improve for the future. While

traditional career goals and financial reward are part of the process in deciding to accept an SIE position, the main desire is

that of an adventure, exploration, and an opportunity for self-

discovery. So, the SIE views the adjustment process as a

learning process, a process that can be managed to a degree by

the self-directed acquisition of information and skillsets that are

attached to the SIE's professional and personal identity. The

SIEs seemed to have a sense of how they contribute to their

social world and that personal sensemaking may be acquired

through gaining tacit knowledge through participative learning.

The SIEs also demonstrated a high degree of critical

thinking and analysis through the practice of what Marsick and

Watkins (2001) termed *reflective practitioner*, the identification

of significant incidental and informal learning opportunities and

the application of reflection on the experience, questioning the

how, the why, and the role of the individual in the experience.

The answers to these questions helped the SIEs in the process of

understanding their identities.

Study participants acknowledged that this process was not

easy or without risk, but they made conscious efforts to find opportunities for increasing their knowledge base through study and interactions within the new environment. Vince, Sutcliffe, and Olivera (2002) discussed the inhibitive power of fear in the development of reflective cultures in organizations. Study participants expressed the presence of these fears in the areas of job security and to slight degrees in personal safety. Participants also indicated that the nature of how the profession was practiced and that leadership and communication issues in the host nation organizations were influential sources of dissatisfaction in the workplace and to a degree in their professional identity. The initial adaptation to the cultural values seemed to result in the loss of professional identify and competence; the SIEs seemed to have established strategies for developing resiliency to compensate for these areas through developing multiple sources of learning opportunities. SIEs adjusted to workplace environments by making a commitment to the learning process and by adapting their values and developing personalized interventions that contributed to their overall self-identity and not specifically to a professional identity. Many participants stated that this ability to adapt in and of itself gave them a level of self-fulfillment and self-actualization. It appears that the reflective learning process contributed to a cycle of cognitive shifts and resiliency that allowed for further seeking self-growth.

Career goals and needs seemed to be centered on feelings and perceptions and not on goals being achieved. This lack of predefined intention may contribute to the vagueness of career motivation but in turn may be a source of resiliency in the freedom and flexibility it allows. There appears to be a duality of the escapee motivational factor rooted in being discontented in the home country career experience, coupled with the sense of adventure and possibility related to the serendipitous event of obtaining the SIE experience. This combination presents unlimited learning possibilities as well as limitless engagement in a boundaryless career as defined by Arthur et al. (2005) and Briscoe et al. (2006). Arabs who could provide insight and knowledge concerning norms and cultural behaviors shared through a common ethnic background and a shared religious belief system. Many of the SIEs reported that this focus became

a gateway to meeting and gaining knowledge with the host locals.

Mendenhall and Oddou (1985) described three levels of

social orientation skills practiced by successfully adjusted expats:

(a) self, (b) others, and (c) perception. The participants in this

study viewed negative interaction experiences not as failures but

as opportunities of feedback to be used in adaptation and

correction as they were learning the intricacies of their new

environment. Ang et al. (2006) found that SIE narratives

conveyed a level of self-efficacy and resilience that was

enhanced by the willingness to ask for help during the adjustment

process. Participants in the present study described the feedback

they received as a change agent that helped them accomplish any

defined goals during the learning process.

The SIE Redefines Professional Identity

Developing multiethnic networks seemed to provide study

participants a higher level of subjective perspective reducing

potential misconceptions, cultural blunders, and segregation.

This cognitive realization of learning helped develop behaviors that allowed for a more comfortable and enjoyable interaction in the new environment. This comfort and enjoyment led to a higher self-efficacy for the SIEs, which gave new energy and motivation to facilitate further learning and lower feelings of threat from failure or mistakes. Frydenberg (1999) stated that coping skills are increased and stress is reduced when individuals perceive they have coping resources. Experiences participants reported seemed to support Frydenberg's contention that each coping success an individual perceives strengthens the development of a new bicultural identity. The SIEs' conscious involvement in their own identity development in turn helped the adjustment process as well in as gaining a sense of success in realizing achievement in the learning process and self-development.

The Psychological Contract

The motivations and personalities of the participants in this study suggest a unique formation of the psychological contract. Rousseau (1989) defined the psychological contract as "an individual's beliefs regarding the terms and conditions of a reciprocal exchange agreement between that focal person and another party" (p. 123), which includes "assumptions regarding good faith, fair dealing, and trust, treating this contract as part of the larger fabric of the relationship between the parties" (p. 128). Rousseau went on to describe how the contract is formed and revised using several stages throughout the life of the employee-employer relationship. Rousseau (2001) later proposed the concept of an individual schema of the employer-employee relationship. Morrison and Robinson (2004) suggested that this schema is determined early in the lifecycle and is deeply tied to the individual's value system and personality. De Vos, Buyens, and Schalk (2003) found that socialization had a positive influence in the shifting or adjustment of this schema. Dulac, Coyle-Shapiro, and Delobbe (2006) reported that the more proactive the individual was in the new environment the faster change would occur.

Thorn (2009) described the SIE as an individual who has abandoned the traditional model of employer-employee and has adopted an autonomy that allows for flexibility and freedom in the control and direction of the individual's career. Parker and Inkson (1999) described SIEs as entrepreneurial and not bound by the traditional concept of career progression. This was supported by Vance (2005,) who reported that SIEs develop a highly intrinsic desire to live and work internationally. From the attitudes of participants in the present study, it appears they make contracts with themselves based on their motivations to initiate the SIE experience, and the return on the investment is measured based on the growth and fulfillment of personal aspirations.

The Continuous Process of Adjustment

Humor. Participants all seemed to have a highly developed sense of humor and were willing to express this directly, often through self-deprecating humor. Hess and Linderman (2007) asserted that humor was a critical element in expats learning to tolerate and adjust when dealing with circumstances that created high levels of frustration, anger, and ambiguity. Humor appears to foster resiliency and a source of strength in dealing with minutiae as well as highly challenging adverse events.

Social media. Social networks played a positive role in the SIE's ability to adjust in terms of terms of social, emotional, and psychological challenges. Study participants all mentioned social media's importance in the adjustment process. Social media also provided a multitude of memberships to communities that in the past may have been outside of the SIE's social circles. Social media provide a vital link of communication to home for SIEs, reducing stress and worry by providing real-time communication. Participants credited this as an important factor in mitigating the sense of loss generated by the distance and separation from their home social circles.

Social media also provided a very valuable avenue in gaining knowledge and contacts SIEs deemed necessary as critical for the learning process. Social networks helped the SIEs gain a sense of belonging to multiple communities and facilitated developing friendships and networks, which SIEs defined as strategically important. Participants reported that the sizeable availability and access to these networks had a very positive influence in the adjustment process. Many participants cited the feeling of control regarding risk, exposure, and safety that access to social networks afforded. Along with providing a connection to loved ones back home, these networks gave SIEs a sense of belonging, acceptance, and emotional satisfaction regarding their development of contacts and involvement with individuals and groups they may otherwise have not come in contact with. The opportunities developed through using these social networks helped eliminate feelings of loneliness and isolation and helped participants explore new avenues of self-growth. The ability to develop and maintain friendships through social networks was reported to positively influence the adjustment process. The participants in the study reported that social networks have also were a viable source of information gathering to help learn and understand local customs, norms, and culture.

The ability to belong to multiple communities through social networking allowed access to a wider knowledge base and contributed to feelings of self-growth, often through the SIE's observational learning. This allowed the SIEs to meet others who share common interests but also allowed a perception of low-risk exposure to things new and unknown. This ability to listen and observe such a large and seemingly unlimited supply of knowledge was a source of empowerment for the SIEs.

An Emerging Model of the SIE Adjustment Process

Data from the present study indicate that the SIE experience is a constant cycle of adjustment and sensemaking and that it is a process that modulates with ebbs and flows. It appears that motivation and personality play major roles in the sensemaking process and influence how SIEs define their psychological contracts concerning the experience. The high self-efficacy and resiliency coupled with the flexible psychological contracts SIEs formed with themselves provided flexibility and resiliency in the sensemaking process and conflict resolution experienced during the adjustment phases. The flexibility afforded by defining the experience as a learning experience and/or as an adventure allowed more flexible expectations and lower frustration regarding the challenge of making sense of conflicts and redefining oneself. Motivational factors and personality also seemed to significantly influence resiliency levels, allowing for a more flexible point of view and a more

internalized locus of control regarding the concept of identity.

Figure 3 shows the cycle and influences of the SIE adjustment

and learning process.

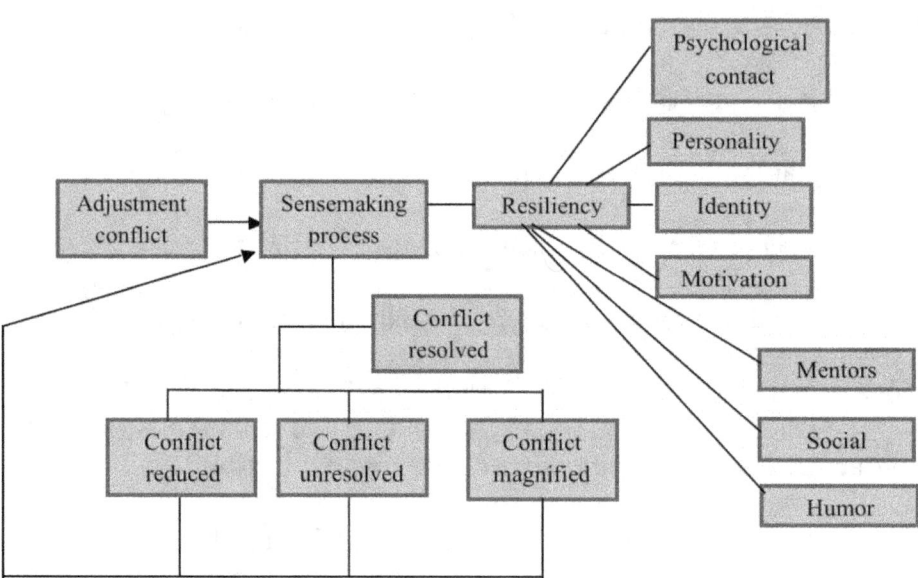

Figure 3. **Model of sensemaking as a lifelong learning process.**

Limitations

This study was limited to SIEs in the education field only,

and the results may not be applicable to traditional multinational

214

corporation expatriates. The small sample size of 32 individuals,

specifically employed in the education sector, created the

possibility that the findings are not generalizable to other career

sector SIEs working in the GCC region and may not be

representative of the population in whole. Also, a very small

number of the participants had families with children, which

previous researchers (Caligiuri et al., 2009; Harvey, 2009; Harvey et

al., 1999) have identified as a major factor of influence regarding

assignment failure rates. A larger study using a larger sample size

may be more beneficial in adding to the knowledge base. Lastly,

as I myself am an SIE, unidentified bias may have limited the

analysis and conclusions despite control factors in the study.

As I am an SIE, I made every effort to ensure that I did

not influence participants' responses to the questions. I did not

share my experiences with participants, and I also avoided

indicating any position regarding my personal opinions or

feelings regarding any circumstances or issues raised during the

interview. It must be acknowledged that the study may contain a

level of unintended bias. I was careful to acknowledge the

possibility of making wrong assumptions based on my prior

knowledge and experience. To counteract this possibility, using

a research journal was instrumental in helping identify areas

where I had personal experiences similar to the participants as

well to ensure that any bias did not influence data analysis.

Implications of the Research for Current Theory

Cartus Research (2012) reported the following

demographics for OEs: 76% male, 71% ages 30 to 49 years, and

69% married. Jokinen et al (2008) reported a shift in these

demographics toward a younger and less career-oriented

population. Participants in the present study support this shift as

the percentages showed markedly changing demographics: 50%

male, 62.4% ages 30 to 49 years, and 46.8% married.

The data regarding SIE career planning and influences

seem to support the metaphorical depiction of a river as described

by Crowley-Henry (2012, p. 139). Inkson et al. (1997) and

Doherty et al. (2011) reported a description of SIEs as having

high personal motivational drives; this description was reinforced

by the responses the present study's participants provided. The role of serendipity and the altruist motivations study participants

described support the definition of the protean career as

expressed by Cerdin and Pargeneux (2010) where the main goal

is completing meaningful work that results in a level of personal

fulfillment and not just a measurement of financial gain. These

results also support findings by Inkson et al. (1997) and Scurry,

Rodriguez, and Bailouni (2013), who describing SIEs as grabbers

of opportunity more than planners of their professional path.

Richardson and McKenna (2002) reported motivational factors of

the desire to explore and to escape from personal/professional

problems as well as the motivation to gain experience for

furthering personal development. The narratives present study

participants provided also support these findings.

The experience's value as an opportunity anchored in the

individual SIE's desire for adventure and level of self-

confidence, family ties, and perception of discontent in one's

current situation is supported by the findings of Richardson and

Mallon (2005), Richardson and McKenna (2002), and Inkson and

Myers (2003), who identified motivators similar to those

described by study participants. Several researchers have also identified and linked the importance of motivational factors as influencing the adjustment process (Berry, 1997; D. T. Hall, 2004; Y. Y. Kim, 2001; Ward, Bochner, & Furnham, 2001). Internationalization's importance and value were also noted as highly influencing factors by Cerdin and Pargneux (2010) and Suutari and Brewster (2000). Data in the present study indicate that the influence of motivational factors and the value of internationalization factors contributed to a higher level of resiliency and impacted the psychological contract developed by the SIE, which in turn can cause individuals to seek out information both formally and informally to complete the sensemaking process.

Black et al. (1991) and Mendenhall and Oddou (1985) defined two distinct categories of expatriate adjustment as psychological adjustment and sociocultural adjustment. Brewster (2002), Donnay (2012), Tharenou and Caulfield (2010) and Yeo et al. (2011) detailed the challenges for SIEs in adjusting to new cultures, languages, religions, and social systems compounded by

the absence of organized systems to offer support. Present study
participants described how they used social media and interaction
with other expatriates to develop and maintain their own
adjustment systems. Experiences and perceptions participants
related revealed the importance of the attitude of a continual
learning process. They also indicated the importance of the SIE
being aware of the adjustment process and using a reflective
learning strategy and the importance of sensemaking related to
changes in behavior and identity. The SIE's commitment,
gaining a level of formal knowledge, and aware and recognizing
informal incidental opportunities are also critical to the
adjustment process.

Olsson (2009) and Weick and Sutcliffe (2005) determined
that experiencing self-fulfillment and exploration offered SIEs
the opportunity to move toward self-actualization. The results of
this study support that concept. The present study's findings also
suggest that how SIEs define the experience is an important
factor in developing the resiliency needed to sustain the
adjustment process. The ability to adapt learning to fit the

219

concept of self-growth as part of one's identity also seemed a critical element for adjustment and success. It could be argued that the SIEs' willingness to allow themselves to learn, adapt, and redefine themselves was a significant factor in adjustment. It should also be noted that most participants were reluctant to define the experience as something that would culminate in either a success or failure. Most simply focused on the experience and what they would keep as they continued their journey after the experience. Fischer et al. (2010) noted that the difference between a good decision and a bad decision as often determined by the influence and balance of one's needs and intuition and a careful analysis of the positive and negative consequences of decision alternatives. The participants in this study indicated that the motivations and their perceptions of their needs being met and the environment meeting the motivational expectations influenced both their decision making process and sensemaking process. The motivations influence the expectations by which the perception of experience is measured against in determining success in the adjustment process.

The present study's implications may be that the definition of success for SIEs may not be concrete. While all study participants are on journeys of self-discovery, and they may share a common belief and value system attributed to the educational profession, each participant is unique and seeking a specific outcome of knowledge. As such, applying a generalizable definition may not be feasible. Much previous research has been focused on attempting to objectively define assessable psychological states as the measurement of success in adjustment. Findings from the present study indicate that the adjustment process is more properly framed as a process of personal change and may be distinct from the individual situation's cognitive context. Adjustment may be facilitated or inhibited by the individual's process of learning and development as well as by managing self-identity, concepts of belonging, and involvement in social networking.

Study findings indicate that the adjustment process is closely linked to the learning process and applying any knowledge gained to the individual's cognitive self-identity. The individual develops a knowledge base to form a psychological contract, which in turn forms mental maps that the individual uses to navigate the circumstances during the sensemaking process. It appears that this personal change is dictated and managed by the individual's attitude and awareness of the process. It also appears that individuals with a high desire for self-growth and new experiences are more likely to experience a positive frame during the adjustment process.

While study participants acknowledged that exposure to the host country culture was limited, this limitation was not considered an impediment to finding opportunities for host country cultural interaction. Observational learning, coupled with using social networks, created opportunities for participants to create self-growth and define their identities. Study participants also seemed to use their perceptions and experiences to develop affirmation in contexts that promoted resiliency and self-growth. Participants acknowledged a level of fear and uncertainty regarding future stability in their professional situation. However, they chose not to focus on the negative possibilities but instead on strategies and opportunities to negate

the chance of loss. Participants also invested energy and

resources in creating the experience of belonging by finding and

joining multiple communities of experience. They were also

willing to reward themselves with positive perceptions and by

acknowledging the impact of even small gains of new

knowledge, skills, and resources regarding their self-concept.

Participants accurately described their self-growth in

relationship to their self-perceptions. While specific goals were

not discussed, the idea or concept of the final overall goal of

mastery as applied to the SIEs' perceptions of their adjustment

levels was often attached to the context of sensemaking. The use

of humor illustrated the participants' awareness of the need to

develop coping mechanisms to help with the emotional aspects of

adjustment and the willingness to not accept the perceived

failures and elements out of their control as defining the final

version of self-identity. Participants exhibited the ability to

manage negative situations and to not allow the common

perceptions attached to such incidents to become problematic for emotional stability and self-efficacy, choosing instead to apply a more positive perspective during the sensemaking process.

Participants reported main sources of frustration directly related to work circumstances, even to the point of professional identity adaptation. The data collected seem to agree with Peltokorpi and Froese's (2009) findings related to the importance of the host environment location and secondary, non-career-motivated interests as a factor in increased adjustment values.

Furthermore the data indicate that the role of personality and the trait of self-efficacy present as significant positive factors in SIE adjustment. Cianni and Tharenou (2000) reported the positive effects of feelings of autonomy related to developing an internal locus of control as well as the higher reports of self-confidence and the abilities to handle any challenge. Participants in this study reported a sense of personal accomplishment and growth when they had perceived to have successfully navigated conflicts during the process. This sense further empowered the participant to believe the next conflict was a new step toward more empowerment and growth. The cycle of increase in self-evaluations of competency and the ability to overcome challenges

that successfully led to higher levels of resiliency described by

present study participants echoed those described by Kimmons

and Greenhaus's (1976) and in greater detail by Betz (2000).

Additionally, the role of relatively stable personality traits has

been indicated as a critical factor in achieving individual success

whether it is personal or career oriented (Costa & McCrae, 1992;

Crockett, 1962). Schmidt and Hunter (1992) stated that increased

perceived competence increases the effort to learn.

SIEs's increased perceptions of autonomy and confidence

and their effect on sensemaking align with Leiba-O'Sullivan's

(1999) findings regarding the role of emotions in the

sensemaking process. Hogan and Shelton (1998) reported that

the more certain SIEs are about their autonomy, the more likely

they are to feel confident regarding future conflict. Findings

from the present study indicate that the sensemaking process is

greatly influenced by motivational factors related to the decision

to expatriate, and that the perceptions in turn influence the

psychological contracts SIEs form. It appears that the identity the SIE defines coupled with the psychological contract allows

for a higher level of resiliency in dealing with the sensemaking

process.

Implications for Practice

For SIEs, adjusting to different and distinct circumstances

in the host country is especially important for adapting to the host

country and new environment. It may be critical for individuals

to know their personality trait makeup before making the

commitment to become an SIE. Adjustment requires the ability

to identify and process uncertainties and anxieties associated with

the SIE process (Mezias & Scandura, 2005). Empirical findings

from studies previously mentioned have suggested the

importance of SIEs being aware of their psychological strengths

and weaknesses in the form of a clear understanding of their

personality construction. Fu, Hsu, and Shaffer (2008) suggested

that such awareness can aid a tactical socialization crucial for

cross-cultural adjustment and adaptation to the host culture. Van

der Zee and Van Oudenhoven (2001) stressed the importance of

the SIE understanding the dynamics in work and nonwork

contexts. Results from other studies have shown the positive effects of cultural flexibility, host country language proficiency, and interpersonal communication skills in developing an understanding of a new culture's dynamics regarding appropriate work values, norms, and standards (Black, 1990; Gudykunst & Nishida, 2001; Mendenhall & Oddou, 1985; Sinangil & Ones, 1997; Takeuchi, Yun, & Russell, 2002).

Of further use may be the application of self-determination theory (Deci & Ryan, 2002) in helping SIEs comprehend and become aware of how motivations behind the decision influence their potential success. Resolved conflicts increase confidence and self-efficacy. Unresolved conflicts become new learning goals and personal challenges or learning situations to be achieved. According to Deci and Ryan (2002), psychological growth is a result of gaining mastery over challenges and taking in new experiences. The engagement with these new challenges and opportunities becomes personalized, and a high level of personal ownership links to the individual's personal values and leads to a more powerful incentive to achieve a resolution. Each resolution then leads to developing a more powerful and competent sense of self for the individual.

Also applicable may be Johns' (2006) research concerning the impact of SIE's psychological need satisfaction and its influence on the SIE's perception of well-being. By being aware of the learning process and making efforts to direct and enhance the process SIEs can mindfully confront, understand, and move toward resolving any perceived conflict. This awareness empowers SIEs in the sensemaking process to a greater understanding of their reality as well as fortifies resilience in preparing for future conflict. This personal growth contributes to greater internal locus of control and higher motivation (Deci & Ryan, 2006). The higher the internal locus of control, the greater the enhancement of the overall experience, which facilitates increased learning and autonomy.

Recommendations for Further Research

Suggestions for further studies would be to test and record personality scales for all participants to see if any consistent or unifying traits can be identified. An area of focus could be on the relationship of Big Five Personality Assessment scores to length of stay. Minimum scores could be indicative of shorter tenure or lower levels of proactive behaviors.

Additionally, a deeper look at the role of social media in specific areas of participants' adjustment process is warranted, including examining the specific types of social media use to determine how much they may have contributed to or decreased resiliency levels as well as enhanced or hindered the sensemaking process. Also, a larger sample with a mixed-method approach including long-term SIEs from other employment sectors may provide a broader and more comprehensive knowledge base concerning the SIE phenomenon in general.

Conclusion

Results from the present study present a variety of themes to add to the current body of literature concerning SIEs. Through examining the narratives of a sample of SIE academics, previous research on SIEs was extended. The data indicate the importance and influence of motivational reasons for choosing to expatriate on the perception of the experience and the sensemaking process of the SIE's adjustment. Some core motivational traits common among SIEs who have been termed successful by completing a minimum of at least one 2-year contract are:

- a sense of adventure,

- self-awareness,

- high self-efficacy,

- proactivity,

- positive self-esteem,

- optimistic orientation, and

- resilience

Study findings indicate agreement with the extant literature in suggesting that the factors influencing the decision to become SIEs are complex but driven more by the desire for adventure and to experience other cultures and not by career ambitions. Career might not be the primary driver but is instead linked and seen as the vehicle through which the adventure can be had. Findings also indicate that the motivational influences seem to overlap or blend into the final decision to relocate.

The narratives shared and examined in the present study offer insight on how individuals learn to adapt to their environment and describe the perceptions and feelings associated with this journey of self-discovery. The participants presented a unique picture of experiences that allowed them to test limits and explore opportunities without restraint and that afforded the opportunity to learn and develop as individuals. The participants described how they became agents of their own development and the architects of their journeys. I sought to contribute important findings on the role of motivation, personality, and resiliency in the sensemaking process of the SIE adjustment experience. Findings showed that the traditional paradigm of the psychological contract has evolved beyond the traditional employee-employer relationship as SIEs are now more entrepreneurial and less traditionally career driven. This supports the need for more research in understanding how the new construct can be used to benefit SIEs and employing organizations.

REFERENCES

Abdalla, I. A., & Al-Homoud, M. A. (2001). Exploring the implicit leadership theory in the Arabian Gulf States. *Applied Psychology: An International Review, 50*, 506–531. http://dx.doi.org/10.1111/1464-0597.00071

Abu-Laghod, L. (2000). *Veiled sentiments: Honour & poetry in a Bedouin society.* Berkley, CA: University of California Press.

Adler, N. J. (1981). Cross-cultural transitions. *Group and Organization Studies, 6*, 342–356. http://dx.doi.org/10.1177/105960118100600310

Adler, N. J. (1984). Women do not want international careers and other myths about international management. *Organizational Dynamics, 13*, 66–79. http://dx.doi.org/10.1016/0090-2616(84)90019-6

Adler, N. J. (1997). *International dimensions of organizational behavior.* Cincinnati, OH: South-Western College Publishing.

Adler, N. J. (2007). *International dimensions of organizational behavior.* Cincinnati, OH: South-Western College Publishing.

Al-Ariss, A. (2010). Modes of engagement, mitigation, self-initiated expatriation and career development. *Career Development International, 15*, 338–358. http://dx.doi.org/10.1177/0149206312441834

Al Bawaba. (2012, February 12). *An unhealthy indicator? GCC heavily dependent on expat workforce.* Retrieved from http://www.albawaba.com

Ali, A. (1995). Cultural discontinuity and Arab management thought. *International Studies of Management and Organization, 25(3)*, 7–30. Retrieved from http://www.tandfonline.com/loi/mimo20#.Vnc7qNb1eCY

Ali A., Taqi, A., & Krishnan, K. (1997). Individualism, collectivism, and decision making styles of managers in Kuwait. *The Journal of Social Psychology, 137*, 629–637. http://dx.doi.org/10.1080/00224549709595484

Al-Kazemi, A. A., & Abbas, J. A., (2002). Managerial problems in Kuwait. *Journal of Management Development, 21*, 366–375. http://dx.doi.org/10.1108/02621710210426853

Allen, N. J., & Meyer, J. P. (1990). The measurement and antecedents of affective, continuance and normative commitment to the organization. *Journal of Occupational Psychology, 63*, 1–18. http://dx.doi.org/10.1111/j.2044-8325.1990.tb00506.x

Al-Rasheedi, S. (2012). *Influence of national culture on employee commitment forms: a case study of Saudi-Western IJVs vs. Saudi domestic companies* (Doctoral thesis, University of Warwick, Coventry, England). Retrieved from http://wrap.warwick.ac.uk/50810/

Alsehan, B. A., Forstenlechner, I. & Al-Nakeeb, A. (2010) Employees' attitudes towards diversity in a non-Western context. *Employees Relations 32*, 42–55. http://dx.doi.org/10.1108/01425451011002752

Altbach, P., & Knight, J. (2007). The internationalization of higher education: Motivations and realities. *Journal of Studies in International Education, 11*, 290–305. http://dx.doi.org/10.1177/1028315307303542

Alvesson, M. A. (2002). *Understanding organizational culture.* London, England: Sage.

Al-Waqfi, M. A. (2012). The antecedents and outcomes of expatriate adjustment of self-initiated expatriates: A theoretical framework. *Academy of Management Proceedings, 1* (Meeting abstract supplement). http://dx.doi.org/10.5465/aomafr.2012.0236

Andersen, R. R., Seibert, R. F., & Wagner, J. G. (2007). *Politics and change in the Middle East: Sources of conflict and accommodation* (8th ed.). Upper Saddle River, NJ: Pearson Prentice Hall.

Anderson, C., Hubona, G., and Al-Gahtani, S. (2007). *Evaluating the antecedents of the technology acceptance model in Saudi Arabia.* Retrieved from http://aisel.aisnet.org/sighci2007/9.

Andreason, A. W. (2003). Direct and indirect forms of in-country support for expatriates and their families as a means of reducing premature returns and improving job performance. *International Journal of Management, 20,* 548–555.

Ang, S., Van Dyne, L., & Koh, C. (2006). Personality correlates of the four-factor model of cultural intelligence. *Group & Organization Management, 31,* 100–123. http://dx.doi.org/10.1177/1059601105275267

Aron, L. (2006). Analytic impasse and the third: Clinical implications of inter-subjectivity theory. *International Journal of Psycho-Analysis, 87,* 349–368. http://dx.doi.org/10.1516/15EL-284Y-7Y26-DHRK

Arthur, M. B., Khapova, S. N., & Wilderon, C. P. M. (2005). Career success in a boundaryless career world. *Journal of Organizational Behavior, 26,* 177–202. http://dx.doi.org/10.1002/job.290

Askary, S., Pounder, J. S., & Yazdifar, H. (2008). Influence of culture on accounting uniformity among Arabic nations. *Education, Business and Society: Contemporary Middle Eastern Issues, 1,* 145–154. http://dx.doi.org/10.1108/17537980810890329

At-Twaijri, M. I., & Al-Muhaiza, I. A. (1996). Hofstede's cultural dimensions in the GCC countries: An empirical investigation. *International Journal of Value-Based Management, 9,* 121–131. http://dx.doi.org/10.1007/BF00440149

Aycan, Z. (1997). Acculturation of expatriate mangers: A process model of adjustment and performance. New approaches to employee management, Expatriate management: Theory and research. In Z. Aycan (Ed.), *New approaches to employee management, Vol. 4: Expatriate management: Theory and research* (pp. 1–40). Greenwich, CT: JAI Press.

Aycan, Z., & Kanungo, R. N. (1997). Current issues and future challenges in expatriate management. In Z. Aycan (Ed.), *New approaches to employee management, Vol. 4: Expatriate management: Theory and research* (pp. 245–260). Greenwich, CT: JAI Press.

Badawy, M. K. (1980). Styles of Mid-Eastern managers. *California Management Review, 22*(2), 51–58. Retrieved from http://cmr.berkeley.edu

Baker, B. (November 2006). *William James, the dilemma of psychical science, and conditions of proof, a post-colonial reading.* Paper presented at the Social Studies of Science Society Annual Meeting, Vancouver, Canada.

Baker, J. C., & Ivancevich, J. M. (1971). The assignment of American executives abroad: Systematic, haphazard or chaotic? *California Management Review, 13*(3), 39–44. http://dx.doi.org/10.2307/41164292

Bakker, B. K. (2009). *The impact of characteristics of expatriation on expatriates, perceived career success* (Doctoral thesis, Utrecht School of Governance Utrecht University,

Utrecht, Netherlands). Retrieved from http:dspace.library.uu.nl/.../Master%20Thesis%20-%20Birke%20Bakker.pdf

Banai, M., & Harry, W. (2004). Boundary-less global careers: The international itinerants. *International Studies of Management and Organization, 34*(3), 96–120. Retrieved from http://www.tandfonline.com/loi/mimo20#.VnWzeNb1e25

Bartlett, C. A., & Ghoshal, S. (1989). *Managing across borders: The transnational solution.* Boston, MA: Harvard Business School Press.

Bartlett, C., Ghoshal, S. & Beamish, P. J. (2007). *Transnational management, text, cases and readings in cross border management* (5th ed.) Burr Ridge, IL: McGraw-Hill/Irwin.

Bass, B. M. (1990). *Bass and Stogdill's handbook of leadership: Theory, research and managerial application* (3rd ed.). New York, NY: Free Press.

Batt, R., & Colvin, A. J. S. (2011). An employment systems approach to turnover: Human resource practices, quits, dismissals, and performance. *Academy of Management Journal, 54*, 695–717. http://dx.doi.org/10.5465/AMJ.2011.64869448

Bennett, R., Aston, A., & Colquhoun, T. (2000). Cross-cultural training: A critical step in ensuring the success of international assignments. *Human Resource Management, 39*, 239–250. http://dx.doi.org/10.1002/1099-050X(200022/23)39:2/3<239::AID-HRM12>3.0.CO;2-J

Berry, J. W. (1997). Immigration, acculturation and adaptation. *Applied Psychology: An International Review, 46*, 1–30. http://dx.doi.org/10.1111/j.1464-0597.1997.tb01087.x

Bertaux, D. (1981). From the life-history approach to the transformation of sociological

practice. In D. Bertaux (Ed.), *Biography and society: The life history approach in the social sciences* (pp. 29–45). London, England: Sage.

Betz, N. E. (2000). Self-efficacy theory as a basis for career assessment. *Journal of Career Assessment, 8*, 205–222. http://dx.doi.org/10.1177/106907270000800301

Bhaskar-Shrinivas, P., Shaffer, M., & Luk, D. (2005). Input-based and time-based models of international adjustment: Meta-analytic evidence and theoretical extensions, *Academy of Management Journal, 48*, 257–281. http://dx.doi.org/10.2307/20159655

Bhawuk, D. P., & Brislin, R. (1992). The measurement of intercultural sensitivity using the concepts of individualism and collectivism. *International Journal of Intercultural Relations, 16*, 413–436. http://dx.doi.org/10.1016/0147-1767(92)90031-O

Bhuiyan, N. I., Paul, D. N. R., & Jabber, M. A. (2002). Feeding the extra millions by 2025–Challenges for rice research and extension in Bangladesh. *Proceedings of the National Workshop on Rice Research and Extension, January 29–31, Gazipur, Bangladesh*, 1–24.

Biemann, T., & Andresen, M. (2010). Self-initiated foreign work experience versus expatriate assignment: A distinct group of international careerists? *Journal of Managerial Psychology, 25*, 430–448. http://dx.doi.org/10.1108/02683941011035313

Birdseye, M. G., & Hill, J. S. (1995). Individual, organizational/work and environmental influences on expatriate turnover tendencies: An empirical study. *Journal of International Business Studies, 26*, 787–813. http://dx.doi.org/10.1057/palgrave.jibs.8490820

234

Bjerke, B., & Al-Meer, A. (1993). Culture's consequences: Management in Saudi Arabia. *Leadership & Organization Development Journal, 14,* 30–35. http://dx.doi.org/10.1108/01437739310032700

Black, B. (1999). National culture and high commitment management. *Employee Relations Journal, 21,* 389–404. http://dx.doi.org/10.1108/01425459910285519

Black, J. S. (1988). Work role transitions: A study of American expatriate managers. *Journal of International Business Studies, 19,* 277–294. Retrieved from http://www.palgrave-journals.com/jibs/index.html

Black, J. S. (1990). The relationship of personal characteristics with adjustment of Japanese expatriate managers. *Management International Review, 30,* 119–134. Retrieved from http://www.springer.com/business+%26+management/journal/11575

Black, J. S., & Gregerson, H. B. (1991). Antecedents to cross-cultural adjustment for expatriates in Pacific Rim assignments. *Human Relations, 44,* 497–515. http://dx.doi.org/10.1177/001872679104400505

Black, J. S., & Gregerson, H. B. (1997). The right way to manage expats. *Harvard Business Review, 77*(2), 5–63. Retrieved from https://hbr.org/1999/03/the-right-way-to-manage-expats

Black, J. S., Gregerson, H. B. & Mendenhall, M. E. (1992). *Global assignments: Successfully expatriating and repatriating international managers.* San Francisco, CA: Jossey-Bass.

Black, J. S., & Mendenhall, M. (1989). A practical but theory-based framework for selecting cross-cultural training methods. *Human Resource Management, 28,* 511–539. http://dx.doi.org/10.1002/hrm.3930280406

Black, J. S., & Mendenhall, M. (1990). Cross-cultural training effectiveness: A review and a theoretical framework for future research. *The Academy of Management Review, 15,* 113–136. http://dx.doi.org/10.5465/AMR.1990.11591834

Black, J. S., Mendenhall, M., & Oddou, G. (1991). Toward a comprehensive model of international adjustment: An integration of multiple theoretical perspectives. *The Academy of Management Review, 16,* 291–317. http://psycnet.apa.org/doi/10.2307/258863

Black, J. S., & Stephens, G. (1989). The influence of the spouse on American expatriate adjustment and intent to stay in Pacific Rim overseas assignments. *Journal of Management, 15,* 529–544. http://dx.doi.org/10.1177/014920638901500403

Black, R. S., Mrasek, K. D., & Ballinger, R. (2003). Individualist and collectivist values in transition for culturally diverse students with special needs. *The Journal for Vocational Special Needs Education, 25*(2/3), 20–29. Retrieved from files.eric.ed.gov/fulltext/EJ854903.pdf

Blakeney, R. N. (August 2006). *Psychological adjustment and sociocultural adaptation: Coping on international assignments.* Paper presented at the annual meeting of the Academy of Management. Atlanta, GA. http://dx.doi.org/10.1007/978-3-8349-9585-8_11

Bonache, J., Brewster, C. & Suutari, V. (2007). Knowledge, international mobility and careers. *International Studies of Management and Organization, 37,* 3–15. http://dx.doi.org/10.2753/IM00020-8825370300

Bond, M. H., Akhtar, H., Ball, P., Bhanthumanavin, D., Boski, P. & Carment, W. (1987). Chinese values and the search for culture-free dimensions of culture. *Journal of Cross-Cultural Psychology, 18,* 143–164. http://dx.doi.org/10.1177/0022002187018002002

Boney, P. K. (2009). *Predicting expatriate adjustment in multi-cultural assignments using the Tilt 360 Leadership Predictor Multi-Source Assessment of Character Strengths* (Doctoral dissertation). Retrieved from http://www.ibrarian.net/navon/paper/Running_head__EXPATRIATE_ADJUSTMENT.pdf?paperid=13166509

Boone, R. S. (1992). Involving culturally diverse parents in transition planning. *Career Development for Exceptional Individuals, 15*, 205–221. http://dx.doi.org/10.1177/088572889201500205

Bossard, A. B., & Peterson, R. B. (2005). The repatriate experience as seen by American expatriates. *Journal of World Business, 40*, 9–28. http://dx.doi.org/10.1016/j.jwb.2004.10.002

Boyacigiller, A., & Adler, N. J. (1991). The parochial dinosaur: Organizational science in a global context. *The Academy of Management Review, 16*, 262–290. http://dx.doi.org/10.5465/AMR.1991.4278936

Bozionelos, N. (2009). Expatriation outside the boundaries of the multinational corporation: A study with expatriate nurses in Saudi Arabia. *Human Resource Management, 48*, 111–134. http://dx.doi.org/10.1002/hrm.20269

Brandl, J., & Neyer, A. K. (2009). Applying cognitive adjustment theory to cross-cultural training for global virtual teams. *Human Resource Management, 48*, 341–353. http://dx.doi.org/10.1002/hrm.20284

Brett, J., Stoh, L. K., & Reilly, A. H. (1992). Job transfer. In C. I. Cooper & I. T. Robinson (Eds.), *International review of industrial and organizational psychology.* (pp. 323–362). London, England: Chichester-Wiley.

Brewster, C. (2002). Human resource practices in multinational enterprises. In M. J. Gannon & K. Newman (Eds.), *The Blackwell handbook of cross-cultural management* (pp. 126–141). Oxford, England: Blackwell.

Brewster, C., Harris, H., & Petrovic, J. (2001). Globally mobile employees: Managing the mix. *Journal of Professional HRM, 25*, 11–15. http://dx.doi.org/10.2753/IMO0020-8825370300

Brewster, C., & Scullion H. (1997). Expatriate HRM: An agenda and a review, *Human Resource Management Journal, 7*, 32–41. http://dx.doi.org/10.1111/j.1748-8583.1997.tb00424.x

Brewster, C., & Suutari, V. (2005). Global HRM: Aspects of a research agenda. *Personnel Review 34*, 5–21. http://dx.doi.org/10.1108/00483480510571851 /00483480510571851

Brien, M., & David, K. (1971). Intercultural communication and the adjustment of the sojourner. *Psychological Bulletin, 76*, 215–230. http://dx.doi.org/10.1037/h0031441

Briody, E. K., & Chrisman, J. B. (1991). Cultural adaptation on overseas assignments. *Human Organization, 50*, 264–280. http://dx.doi.org/10.17730/humo.50.3.22555451v6206444

Briscoe, J. P., Hall, D. T., & Frautschy-DeMuth, R. L. (2006). Protean and boundary less careers: An empirical exploration. *Journal of Vocational Behavior, 69*, 30–47. http://dx.doi.org/10.1016/j.jvb.2005.09.003

Brislin, R. W. (1981). *Cross-cultural encounters.* New York, NY: Pergamon Press.

Brislin, R. W., Lommer, W. J., & Thorndike, R. M. (1973). *Cross-cultural research methods.* New York, NY: Wiley.

Brookfield Global Relocation Services. (2010). *Global relocation trends survey 2010*. Retrieved from https://espritgloballearning.com/wp-content/uploads/2011/03/2010_GlblReloTrendsSurvey.pdf

Brown, A. (1995). *Organizational culture* (2nd ed.). Harlow, England: Pearson.

Bruggeman, S. (2010). A *knowledge integration perspective on the study of self-initiated expatriates* (Doctoral thesis, Henley Business School/University of Reading, Greenlands, Henley-on-Thames, Oxfordshire, United Kingdom). Retrieved form http://ethos.bl.uk/uk.bl.ethos.528231/

Bryman, A. (2008). *Social research methods* (3rd ed.). Oxford, England: Oxford University Press

Burnett, M. F., Williamson, I. O., & Bartol, K. M. (2009). The moderating effect of personality on employees' reactions to procedural fairness and outcome favorability. *Journal of Business and Psychology, 24*, 469–484. http://dx.doi.org/10.1007/s/0869-009-6

Caligiuri, P. M. (2000a). The Big Five personality characteristics as predictors of expatriate's desire to terminate the assignment and supervisor-rated performance. *Personnel Psychology, 53*, 67–88. http://dx.doi.org/10.1111/j.1744-6570.2000.tb00194.x

Caligiuri, P. M. (2000b). Selecting expatriates for personality characteristics: A moderating effect of personality on the relationship between host national contact and cross-cultural adjustment. *Management International Review, 40*, 61–80. Retrieved from http://www.springer.com/business+%26+management/journal/11575

Caligiuri, P., & Colakoglu, S. (2007). A strategic contingency approach to expatriate assignment management. *Human Resource Management Journal, 17*, 393–410. http://dx.doi.org/10.1111/j.1748-8583.2007.00052.x

Caligiuri, P., & Tarique, I. (2009). Predicting effectiveness in global leadership activities. *Journal of World Business, 44*, 336–346. http://dx.doi.org/10.1016/j.jwb.2008.11.005

Caligiuri, P., Tarique, I., & Jacobs, R. (2009). Selection for international assignments. *Human Resource Management Review, 19*, 251–262. Retrieved from http://www.journals.elsevier.com/human-resource-management-review/

Capellen, T., & Janssens, M. (2005). Career paths of global managers: Towards future research. *Journal of World Business, 40*, 348–360. http://dx.doi.org/10.1016/j.jwb.2005.08.003

Cartus Research (2012). *Global trends survey, greatest challenges*. Retrieved from http://guidance.cartusrelocation.com/research-and-trends.html

Cavaleri, S., & Reed, F. (2008). Leading dynamically complex projects. *International Journal of Managing Projects in Business, 1*, 71–87. http://dx.doi.org/10.1108/17538370810846423

Cerdin, J.-L., & Pargneux, M. L. (2010). Career anchors: A comparison between organization-assigned and self-initiated expatriates, *Thunderbird International Business Review, 52*, 287–299. http://dx.doi.org/10.1002/tie.20350

Chen, Y. P., (2012). *A three-stage process model of self-initiated expatriate career transitions: A self-determination theory perspective* (Doctoral dissertation). Available from ProQuest Dissertations and Theses database. (UMI No. 3523920)

Cheuk, B. (2008). Delivering business value through information literacy in the workplace. *Libri, 57*, 137–143. http://dx.doi.org/10.1515/libr.2008.015

Church, A. (1982). Sojourner adjustment. *Psychological Bulletin, 9*, 540–572. http://dx.doi.org/10.1037/0033-2909.91.3.540

Cianni, M., & Tharenou, P. (2000). A cross-cultural study of the willingness of graduating students to accept expatriate assignments. In R. Edwards, C. Nyland & M. Coulhard (Eds.), *Readings in international business* (pp. 159–177). St. Paul, MN: West.

Cohen, A. (2006). The relationship between multiple commitments and organizational citizenship behaviour in Arab and Jewish culture. *Journal of Vocational Behaviour, 69*, 105–118. http://dx.doi.org/10.1016/j.jvb.2005.12.004

Cohen, D. J., & Crabtree, B. J. (2006). *Qualitative research guidelines project.* Retrieved from http://www.qualres.org/

Cohen, E. (1977). Expatriate communities. *Current Sociology, 24*, 5–129. http://dx.doi.org/10.1177/001139217702400301

Collings, D. G., Scullion, H., & Morley, M. J. (2007). Changing patterns of global staffing in the multinational enterprise: Challenges to the conventional expatriate assignment and emerging alternatives. *Journal of World Business, 42*, 198–213. http://dx.doi.org/10.1016/j.jwb.2007.02.005

Connelly, B., Hitt, M. A., DeNisi, A. S., & Ireland, R. D. (2007). Expatriates and corporate-level international strategy: Governing with the knowledge contract. *Management Decision, 45*, 564–578. Retrieved from http://ssrn.com/abstract=1374694

Conrad, P. (1987). The experience of illness: Recent and new directions. *Research in the Sociology of Health Care, 6*, 1–31. Retrieved from http://www.emeraldinsight.com/series/rshc

Cooper, D. R., & Schindler, P. S. (2006). *Business research methods* (9th ed.). New York, NY: McGraw-Hill.

Coopey, J., & Hartley, J. (1991). Reconsidering the case for organizational commitment *Human Resource Management Journal, 1*, 18–32. http://dx.doi.org/10.1111/j.1748-8583.1991.tb00228.x

Costa, P. T., Jr., & McRae, R. R. (1992). *Revised NEO Personality Inventory (NEO-PI-R) and NEO Five-Factor Inventory (NEO-FFI) professional manual.* Odessa, Florida: Psychological Assessment Resources.

Coyle, W. L. (1986). *The impact of relocation on the wives of transferred executives* (Unpublished master's thesis). Retrieved from repub.eur.nl/.../LG%20%20PhD%20manuscript%20Publish%20%20%20

Creswell, J. (1998). *Qualitative inquiry and research design: Choosing among five traditions.* Thousand Oaks, CA: Sage.

Creswell, J. W. (2003). *Research design: Qualitative, quantitative and mixed methods approaches.* London, England: Sage.

Creswell, J. W. (2005). *Educational research: Planning, conducting, and evaluating quantitative and qualitative research* (2nd ed.). Upper Saddle River, NJ: Pearson.

Creswell, J.W. (2007). *Qualitative inquiry and research design: Choosing among five approaches* (2nd ed.). Thousand Oaks, CA: Sage.

Creswell, J. W. (2009). Research *design: Qualitative, quantitative, and mixed methods approaches* (3rd ed.). Los Angeles, CA: Sage.

Crockett, H. J. (1962). The achievement motive and differential occupational mobility in the United States. *American Sociological Review, 27*, 191–204. http://dx.doi.org/10.2307/2089675

238

Crouch, M., & McKenzie, H. (2006). The logic of small samples in interview based qualitative research. *Social Science Information, 45*, 483–499. http://dx.doi.org/10.1177/0539018406069584

Crowley-Henry, M. (2007). The protean career: Exemplified by first world foreign residents in Western Europe? *International Studies of Management & Organization, 37*, 44–46. http://dx.doi.org/10.2753/IMO0020-8825370302

Deci, E. L., & Ryan, R. M. (2002). The paradox of achievement: The harder you push, the worse it gets. In J. Aronson (Ed.), *Improving academic achievement: Impact of psychological factors on education* (pp. 61–87). San Diego, CA: Academic Press.

Denny, F. M. (2005). *Introduction to Islam*. London, England: Prentice Hall.

Denzin, N. K. (1989). *Interpretive biography*. Newbury Park, CA: Sage.

Dervin, B. (1998). Sense-making theory and practice: An overview of user interests in knowledge seeking and use. *Journal of Knowledge Management, 2*(2), 36–46. http://dx.doi.org/10.1108/13673279810249369

De Vos, A., Buyens, D., & Schalk, R. (2003). Psychological contract development during organizational socialization: Adaptation to reality and the role of reciprocity. *Journal of Organizational Behavior, 24*, 537–559. http://dx.doi.org/10.1002/job205

Dickmann, M., & Harris, H. (2005). Developing career capital for global career: The role of international assignments. *Journal of World Business, 40*, 399–408. http://dx.doi.org/10.1016/j.jwb.2005.08.007

Digman, J. M. (1990). Personality structure: Emergence of the five-factor model. *Annual Review of Psychology, 41*, 417–440. http://dx.doi.org/10.1146/annurev.ps.41.020190.002221

Dirani, K. M. (2008). Individualism and collectivism in Lebanon: Correlations with socioeconomic factors and effects on management and human resource practices. *Advances in International Management, 21*, 211–233. http://dx.doi.org/10.1016/S1571-5027(08)00009-0

Doherty, N., Dickmann, M & Mills, T. (2011). Exploring the motives of company-backed and self-initiated expatriates. *International Journal of Human Resource Management, 22*, 595–611. http://dx.doi.org/10.1080/09585192.2011.543637

Donnay, S. (2012). *Intercultural competencies and self-initiated expatriates' self-perceived effectiveness: A case study of European expatriates in Brussels* (Unpublished master's thesis). Retrieved from no.uvt.nl/show.cgi?fid=127379

Dowling, P. J., & Welch, D. E. (2004). *International human resource management: Managing people in an international context* (4th ed.). London, England: Thompson.

Doz, Y., & Prahalad, C. K. (1986). Controlled variety: A challenge for human resource management in the MNC. *Human Resource Management, 25*, 55–71. http://dx.doi.org/10.1002/hrm.3930250105

Drlíková, E. (1992). *Učiteľská psychológia*. Bratislava, Slovakia: SPN. Drlíková, E. (1992). *Učiteľská psychológia*. Bratislava, Slovakia: SPN

Dube, A., Freeman, E., & Reich, M. (2010). *Employee replacement costs*. Retrieved from www.irle.berkeley.edu/201-10.pdf

Duckett, B. (1999). The Blackwell Encyclopedic Dictionary of Human Resource Management [Review of the book *The Blackwell encyclopedic dictionary of human resource management*]. *Reference Reviews, 13*(3), 24–25. Retrieved from http://www.emeraldinsight.com/loi/rr

Dulac, T., Coyle-Shapiro, J. A-M., & Delobbe, N. (June 2006). *The role of socialization tactics and information seeking behavior in newcomers' psychological contract evaluation*. Paper presented at the annual meeting of the Academy of Management, Atlanta, Georgia. http://dx.doi.org/10.1.1335.5072

Earley, P. C., & Ang, S. (2003). *Cultural intelligence: Individual interactions across cultures*. Palo Alto, CA: Stanford University Press.

Ellingsworth, H. W. (1983). Adaptive intercultural communication. In W. B. Gudykunst & Y. Y. Kim (Eds.), *Intercultural communication theory: Current perspectives* (pp. 195–204). Beverly Hills, CA: Sage.

Ellison, C. M., Boykin, A. W., Towns, D. P., & Stokes, A. (2000). *Classroom cultural ecology: The dynamics of classroom life in schools serving low-income African-American children* (Rep. No. 44). Washington, DC: Center for Research on the Education of Students Placed At Risk.

Fermelis, J. (January 2011). Australian expatriates in Shanghai: Generation Y emerges. *Proceedings of the 76th Annual Convention of the Association for Business Communication, 19–22, 2011–Montreal, Quebec, Canada* Retrieved from http://dro.deakin.edu.au/view/DU:30040202?print_friendly=true

Finlay, L., & Gough, B. (2008). *Reflexivity: A practical guide for researchers in health and social sciences*. Oxford, England: Blackwell.

Fischer, P., Fischer, J., Weisweiler, S., & Frey, D. (2010). Selective exposure to information: How different modes of decision making affect subsequent confirmatory information processing. *British Journal of Social Psychology, 49*, 871–881. http://dx.doi.org/10.1348/014466610X499668

Fitzgerald, C., & Howe-Walsh, L. (2008). Self-initiated expatriates: An interpretative phenomenological analysis of professional female expatriates. *International Journal of Business and Management, 3*, 156–175. http://dx.doi.org/10.5539/ijbm.v3n10p156

Fontana, A., & Frey, J. H. (2003). The interview: From structured questions to negotiated text. In K. Denzin & Y. S. Lincoln (Eds.), *Collecting and interpreting qualitative materials* (pp. 61–106). Thousand Oaks, CA: Sage.

Forseth-Whitman, M., & Isakovic, A.A. (2012). Can personality traits influence international experience success and stress management strategies of organizational and self-initiating expatriates? *The Journal of Global Business Management, 8*, 102–110. Retrieved from www.jgbm.org/page/14%20Mary%20Whitman.pdf

240

Forster, N. (1994). The forgotten employee? The experiences of expatriate staff returning to the UK. *The International Journal of Human Resources Management, 5*, 405–425. http://dx.doi.org/10.1080/09585199400000024

Forster, N. (1997). The persistent myth of high expatriate failure rate: A reappraisal. *International Journal of Human Resource Management, 8*, 414–433. http://dx.doi.org/10.1080/095851997341531

Forster, N. (2000a). Expatriates and the impact of cross cultural training. *Human Resource Management Journal, 10*, 63–78. http://dx.doi.org/10.1111/j.1748-8583.2000.tb00027.x.

Forster, N. (2000b). *Managing staff on international assignments: A strategic guide.* London, England: Financial Times/Prentice Hall.

Fougere, M., & Moulettes, A. (2006). Development and modernity in Hofstede's Culture's Consequences: A postcolonial reading. *Lund Working Paper Series, 2006.* Retrieved from www.lunduniversity.lu.se/lup/publication/1387511

Foust-Cummings, H., L. Sabattini, G, & Carter, N. (2008). *Women in technology: Maximizing talent, minimizing barriers.* New York, NY: Catalyst.

Francesco, A. M., & Gold, B. A. (1998). *International organizational behaviour* (2nd ed.). Upper Saddle River, NJ: Pearson.

Frydenberg, E. (1999). Understanding coping: Towards a comprehensive theoretical framework. In E. Frydenberg (Ed.), *Learning to cope: Developing as a person in complex societies* (pp. 248–273). New York, NY: Oxford University Press.

Fu, C. K., Hsu, Y. S., & Shaffer, M. A. (2008). Socialization tactics, fit and expatriate outcomes. *The Academy of Management Best Paper Proceedings* (pp. 1-6). Retrieved from www.proceedings.aom.org/content/2008/1/1.238.full.pdf

Furnham, A. (1988). The adjustment of sojourners. In Y. Y. Kim & W. B. Gudykunst (Eds.), *Cross-cultural adaptation: Current approaches* (pp. 42–62). Newbury Park, CA: Sage.

Gilbert, D., & Tsao, J. (2000). Exploring Chinese cultural influences and hospitality marketing relationships. *International Journal of Contemporary Hospitality Management, 12*, 45–53. http://dx.doi.org/10.1108/09596110010305037

Gillham, B. (2000). *Case study research methods.* London, England: Continuum.

Gilly, M. C. (1995). Session overview consumer acculturation: Immigrant, migrants and expatriates. *Advances in Consumer Research, 22*, 505. Retrieved from http://acrwebsite.org/volumes/7797/volumes/v22/NA-22

Giorgi, A. (2008). Concerning a serious misunderstanding of the essence of the phenomenological method in psychology. *Journal of Phenomenological Psychology, 39*, 33–58. http://dx.doi.org/10.1163/156916208X311610

Glanz, L., & van der Sluis, E. C. (2001). Employing organisations and expatriate spouses: Balancing self-knowledge and knowledge about options. *Career Development International, 6*, 169–176. http://dx.doi.org/10.1108/13620430110389757

Glaser, B., & Strauss, A. (1967). *The discovery of grounded theory: Strategies for qualitative research.* New York, NY: Aldine.

Goffman, E. (1966). *Behavior in public places: Notes on the social organization of gatherings.* New York, NY: The Free Press.

Graneheim U. H., & Lundman B. (2004). Qualitative content analysis in nursing research: Concepts, procedures and measures to achieve trustworthiness. *Nurse Education Today, 24*, 105–112. http://dx.doi.org/10.1016/j.nedt.2003.10.001

Green, E. G. T., Deschamps, J., & Paez, D. (2005). Variations of individualism and collectivism within and between 20 countries. *Journal of Cross-Cultural Psychology, 36*, 321–339. http://dx.doi.org/10.1177/0022022104273654

Greenfield, P. M., Trumbull, E., Keller, H., Rothstein-Fisch, C., Suzuki, L. K., & Quiroz, B. (2006). *Cultural conceptions of learning and development.* In P. A. Alexander & P. H. Winne (Eds.), *Handbook of educational psychology* (2nd ed., pp. 675–692). Mahwah, NJ: Erlbaum.

Gregerson, H. B., & Black, S. (1990). A multifaceted approach to expatriate retention in international assignments. *Group & Organization Studies, 15*, 461–485. http://dx.doi.org/10.1177/105960119001500409

Gudykunst, W., & Nishida, T. (2001). Anxiety, uncertainty, and perceived effectiveness of communication across relationships and cultures. *International Journal of Intercultural Relations, 25*, 55–71. http://dx.doi.org/10.1016/S0147-1767(00)00042-0

Guest, G., Bunce, A., & Johnson, L., (2006). How many interviews are enough? An experiment with data saturation and variability. *Field Methods, 18*(1), 59–82. http://dx.doi.org/10.1177/1525822X05279903

Gullahorn, J. T., & Gullahorn J. E. (1963). An extension of the U-curve hypothesis. *Journal of Social Issues, 19*, 33–47. http://dx.doi.org/10.1111/j.1540-4560.1963.tb00447.x

Gupta, A. K., & Govindarajan, V. (1991). Knowledge flows and the structure of control within multinational corporations. *Academy of Management Review, 16*, 768–792. Retrieved from http://aom.org/Publications/AMR/Academy-of-Management-Review.aspx

Guthrie, G. M., & Zektick, I. N. (1967). Predicting performance in the Peace Corps. *Journal of Social Psychology, 71,* 11–21. http://dx.doi.org/10.1080/00224545.1967.9919761

Guthrie, J. P., Ash, R. A., & Stevens, C. D. (2003). Are women better than men? Personality differences and expatriate selection. *Journal of Managerial   Psychology, 18*, 229–243. http://dx.doi.org/10.1108/02683940310465243

Hailey J. (1996). The expatriate myth: Cross-cultural perceptions of expatriate managers. *International Executive, 38*, 188–658. http://dx.doi.org/10.1002/tie.5060380206

Hall, D. (1976). Protean careers of the 21st century. *The Academy of Management Executive, 19*(4), 8–16. Retrieved from http://www.jstor.org/journal/acadmanaexe2

Hall, D. T. (2004). The protean career: A quarter-century journey, *Journal of Vocational Behavior, 65*, 1–13. http://dx.doi.org/10.1016/j.jvb.2003.10.006

Hall, E. T. (1992). *Anthropology of everyday life: An autobiography.* New York, NY: Doubleday.

Hall, M. R., & Hall, E. T. (1975). *The fourth dimension in architecture: The impact of building on behavior.* Santa Fe, NM: Sunstone Press.

Harris, H. (1995). Women's role in international management. In A. W. K. Harzing & J. Van Ruysseveldt (Eds.), *International human resource management* (pp. 26–31). London, England: Sage.

Harris, H. (1999). Women in international management: Why are they not selected? In C. Brewster & H. Harris (Eds.), *International HRM: Contemporary issues in Europe* (pp. 459–76). London, England: Routledge.

Harris, J. E. (1989). Moving managers internationally: The care and feeding of expatriates. *Human Resource Planning, 12*, 49–53.

Harrison, D., & Shaffer, M. (2005). Mapping the criterion space for expatriate success: Task-and relationship-based performance, effort and adaptation. *International Journal of Human Resource Management, 16*, 1454–1474. http://dx.doi.org/10.1080/09585190500220648

Harvey M. G. (1985). The executive family: An overlooked variable in international assignments. *Colombia Journal of World Business, 20*, 84–93. http://dx.doi.org/10.1002/tie.5060270307

Harvey, M., Buckley, M. R., Novicevic, M. M., & Wiese, D. (1999). Mentoring dual career expatriates: A sensemaking and self-managing social support process. *International Journal of Human Resource Management, 10*, 808–827. http://dx.doi.org/10.1111/j.1559-1816.2009.00571.x

Haslberger, A. (2005). Facets and dimensions of cross-cultural adaptation: Refining the tools. *Personnel Review, 34*, 85–109. http://dx.doi.org/10.1108/00483480510571897

Haslberger, A. (2008). The complexities of expatriate adaptation, *Human Resource Management Review, 15*, 160–180. http://dx.doi.org/10.1016/j.hrmr.2005.07.001

Haslberger, A., & Brewster, C. (2007, May). *Domains of expatriate adjustment with special emphasis on work.* Paper presented at the Cadiz University's VI. International Workshop on Human Resource Management, Jerez, Spain. Retrieved from https://ashridge.org.uk/DomainsOfExpatriateadjustmentwithspecialemphasisonwork[1].pdf

Hassan, O.A. (30 March, 2015) The GCC's Formation: The Official Version. *Al Jazeera Center for Studies.* Mecca, Saudi Arabia.

http://studies.aljazeera.net/en/dossiers/2015/03/201533011258831763.html.

Hechanova, R., Beehr, T. A., & Christiansen, N. D. (2003). Antecedents and consequences of employees' adjustment to overseas assignment: A meta analytic review. *Applied Psychology, 52*, 213–236. http://dx.doi.org/10.1111/1464-0597.00132

Hegel, G. W. F. (1977). *Phenomenology of spirit.* (A. V. Miller, Trans., J. N. Findlay, Analysis). Oxford, United Kingdom: Oxford University Press.

Heidegger, M. (1962). *Being and time.* (J. Macquarrie & E. Robinson, Trans.). New York, NY: Harper. (Original work published 1927).

Hess, M., & Linderman, P. (2007). *The expert expatriate.* Boston, MA: Intercultural Press.

Hickson, D. J., & Pugh, D. S. (1995). *Management worldwide: The impact of societal culture on organizations around the globe.* London, England: Penguin Books.

Hill, C.W.L. (2003). *International business: Competing in the global market place* (4th ed.) Boston, MA: McGraw-Hill

Hill, P. C. (2005). Measurement in the psychology of religion and spirituality: Current status and evaluation. In R. F. Paloutzian & C. L. Park (Eds.), *Handbook of the psychology of religion and spirituality* (pp. 48–74). New York, NY: Guilford Press.

Hipsher, S. (2008). *Expatriates in Asia: Breaking free from the colonial paradigm.* Oxford, England: Chandos.

Hofstede, G. (1980). *Culture's consequences: International differences in work-related values.* Beverly Hills, CA: Sage.

Hofstede, G. (1991). *Cultures and organizations: Software of the mind.* London, England: McGraw-Hill.

Hofstede G. (1998). Attitudes, values and organizational culture: Disentangling the concepts. *Organization Studies, 19*, 477–493. http://dx.doi.org/10.1177/017084069801900305

Hofstede, G. (2001). *Cultures consequence: Comparing values, behaviors, institutions and organizations across nations* (2nd ed.). London, England: Sage.

Hofstede, G. (2007). Asian management in the 21st century. *Asia Pacific Journal of Management, 24*, 411–420. http://dx.doi.org/10.1007/s10490-007-9049-0

Hofstede, G., & Bond, M. H. (1991). The Confucius connection: From cultural roots to economic growth. *Organizational Dynamics, 16*, 4–21. http://dx.doi.org/10.1016/0090-2616(88)90009-5

Hofstede, G., Hofstede, J. G., & Minkov, M., (2010). *Cultures and organizations: Software of the mind* (3rd ed.). New York, NY: McGraw-Hill.

Hofstede, G., & Usuniers, J. C., (1996). Hofstede's dimensions of culture and their influence on international business negotiations. In P. Ghauri & J. C. Usunier (Eds.), *International business negotiations* (pp. 119–130). Oxford, England: Elsevier.

The Hofstede Centre. (n.d.). National culture. Retrieved from http://geert-hofstede.com/national-culture.html

Hogan, R., & Shelton, D. (1998). A socioanalytic perspective on job performance. *Human Performance, 11*, 129–144. http://dx.doi.org/10.1080/08959285.1998.9668028

Holopainen, J., & Björkman, I. (2005). The personal characteristics of the successful expatriate: A critical review of the literature and an empirical investigation. *Personnel Review, 34*, 37–50. http://dx.doi.org/10.1108/00483480510578476

Hoppe, M. H. (1990). *A comparative study of country elites: International differences in work-related values and learning and their implications for management training and development* (Unpublished doctoral dissertation). Chapel Hill, University of North Carolina at Chapel Hill.

House, J. R., Hanges J. P., Mansour, J., Dorfman, J. P., & Gupta, V. (2004). *Culture, leadership and organizations: Illustrative examples of GLOBE findings.* Thousand Oaks, CA: Sage.

Howe-Walsh, L., & Schyns, B. (2010). Self-initiated expatriation: Implications for HRM. *The International Journal of Human Resource Management, 21*, 260–273. http://dx.doi.org/10.1080/09585190903509571

Hoyt, W. T. & Bhati, K. S. (2007). Principles and practices: An empirical examination of qualitative research in the *Journal of Counseling Psychology. Journal of Counseling Psychology, 54*, 201–210. http://dx.doi.org/10.1037/0022-0167.54.2.201

Huang, T. J., Chi, S. C., & Lawler, J. J. (2005). The relationship between expatriates' personality traits and their adjustment to international assignments. *The International Journal of Human Resource Management, 16*, 1656–1670. http://dx.doi.org/10.1080/09585190500239325

Hui, C. H., Triandis, H. C., & Yee, C. (1991). Cultural differences in reward allocation: Is collectivism the explanation? *British Journal of Social Psychology, 30*, 145–157. http://dx.doi.org/10.1111/j.2044-8309.1991.tb00931.x

Husserl, E. (1970). *The crisis of European sciences and transcendental phenomenology.* Evanston, IL: Northwestern University Press. (Original work published 1936).

Inkson, K. (1997). Organization structure and the transformation of careers. In T. Clark (Ed.), *Advancement in organizational behavior* (pp. 165–185). Aldershot, United Kingdom: Ashgate.

Inkson, K., & Myers, B. A. (2003). The big OE: Self-directed travel and career development. *Career Development International, 8*, 170–181. http://dx.doi.org/10.1108/13620430310482553

Inkson, K., Arthur, M., Pringle, J., & Barry, S. (1997). Expatriate assignment versus overseas experience: Contrasting models of international human resource development. *Journal of World Business, 32*, 351–368. http://dx.doi.org/10.1016/S1090-9516(97)90017-1

International Labour Organization. (2013). *Global employment trends 2013: Recovering from a second jobs dip.* Retrieved from http://www.ilo.org/wcmsp5/groups/public/---dgreports/---dcomm/---publ/documents/publication/wcms_202326.pdf.

Jacoby, S. M., Nason, E. M., & Saguchi, K. (2005). Corporate organization in Japan and the United States: Is there evidence of convergence? *Social Science Japan Journal, 8*, 43–67. http://dx.doi.org/10.2139/ssrn.559124

Jandt, F. E. (2004). *Intercultural communication: An introduction* (4th ed.). London, England: Sage.

Javidan, M., Dorfman, P. W., Sulley de Luque, M., & House, R. J. (2006). In the eye of the beholder: Cross-cultural lessons in leadership from Project GLOBE. *Academy of Management Perspectives, 20*, 67–90. http://dx.doi.org/10.5465/AMP.2006.19873410

John, O. P., Donahue, E. M., & Kentle, R. L. (1991). *The Big Five Inventory–Versions 4a and 54.* Berkeley: University of California, Berkeley, Institute of Personality and Social Research.

John, O. P., & Srivastava, S. (1999). The Big-Five trait taxonomy: History, measurement, and theoretical perspectives. In L. A. Pervin & O. P. John (Eds.), *Handbook of personality: Theory and research* (Vol. 2, pp. 102–138). New York, NY: Guilford Press.

Johns, C. (2006). *Engaging reflection in practice: A narrative approach.* Oxford, England: Blackwell.

Jokinen, T., Brewster, C., & Sutari, V. (2008). Career capital during international work experiences: Contrasting self-initiated expatriate experiences and assigned expatriation. *The International Journal of Human Resource Management, 19*, 979–998. http://dx.doi.org/10.1080/09585190802051279

Kačáni, V. (2004). *Základy učiteľskej psychológie.* Bratislava, Slovakia: SPN

Kale, S. (1996). How national culture, organizational culture and personality impact buyer-seller interactions. In P. Ghauri & J. C. Usunier (Eds.), *International business negotiations* (pp. 21–38). Oxford, England: Elsevier.

Kalliny, M., Cruthirds, K. W., & Minor, M. S. (2006). Differences between American, Egyptian and Lebanese humor styles: Implications for international management. *International Journal of Cross Cultural Management, 6*, 121–134. http://dx.doi.org/10.1177/1470595806062354

Kanter, R. M. (1993). *Men and women of the corporation.* New York, NY: Basic Books.

Kassem, M. S., & Habib, G. M. (1989). *Strategic management of services in the Arab Gulf States: Company and industry cases.* Berlin, Germany: W. de Gruyter.

Kealey, D., Protheroe, D., MacDonald, D., & Vulpe, T. (2005). International projects: Some lessons on avoiding failure and maximizing success. *Performance Improvement, 45*, 38–46. http://dx.doi.org/10.1002/pfi.2006.4930450309

245

Keohane, R. O. (2003). The concept of accountability in world politics and the use of force. *Michigan Journal of International Law, 24*, 1–21. Retrieved from http://www.mjilonline.org

Kim, K., & Slocum, J. W. (2008). Individual differences and expatriate assignment effectiveness: The case of U.S.-based Korean expatriates. *Journal of World Business, 43*, 109–126. http://dx.doi.org/10.1016/j.jwb.2007.10.005

Kim, Y. Y. (2001). *Becoming intercultural: An integrative theory of communication and cross-cultural adaptation*. Thousand Oaks, CA: Sage.

Kimmons, G., & Greenhaus, J. H. (1976). Relationship between locus of control and reactions of employees to work characteristics, *Psychological Reports, 39*, 815–820. http://dx.doi.org/10.2466/pr0.1976.39.3.815

Kitzinger, J. (1995). Qualitative research: Introducing focus groups. *BMJ, 311*, 299–302. http://dx.doi.org/10.1136/bmj.311.7000.299

Klaff, L. G. (2002). The right way to bring expats home. *Workforce, 81*, 40–44. Retrieved from http://www.workforce.com/articles/the-right-way-to-bring-expats-home

Klein, A. (1998). Firm performance and board committee structure. *Journal of Law & Economics, 41*, 275–303. http://dx.doi.org/10.1086/467391

Klein, A., Waxin, M. F., & Radnell, E. (2009). The impact of the Arab national culture on the perception of ideal organizational culture in the United Arab Emirates: An empirical study of 17 firms. *Education, Business and Society: Contemporary Middle Eastern Issues, 2*, 44–56. http://dx.doi.org/10.1108/17537980910938479

Kluckhohn, F. R., & Strodtbeck, F. L. (1961). *Variations in value orientations*. New York, NY: Row, Peterson.

Kohonen, E. (2005). Developing global leaders through international assignments: An identity constructing perspective. *Personnel Review, 34*, 22–36. http://dx.doi.org/10.1108/00483480510571860

Kollinger, I. (2007). Women and expatriate work opportunities in Austrian organizations. *The International Journal of Human Resource Management, 6*, 1243–1260. http://dx.doi.org/10.1080/09585190500144186

Kraimer, M. L., & Wayne, S. J. (2004). An examination perceived organizational support as a multidimensional construct in the context of an expatriate assignment. *Journal of Management, 30*, 209–237. http://dx.doi.org/10.1016/j.jm.2003.01.001

Kreitner, R., & Kinicki, A. (1998). *Organizational behavior* (4th ed.). Berkshire, England: McGraw-Hill.

Kupka, B., Everett, A., & Cathro, V. (2008). Home alone and often unprepared—Intercultural communication training for expatriated partners in German MNCs. *The International Journal of Human Resource Management, 19*, 1765–1791. http://dx.doi.org/10.1080/09585190802323819

Lee, H. W. (2007). Factors that influence expatriate failure: An interview study. *International Journal of Management, 24*, 403–415.

Lee, L. Y., & Croker, R. (2006) A contingency model to promote the effectiveness of expatriate training. *Industrial Management + Data Systems, 106*, 1187–1205. http://dx.doi.org/10.1108/02635570610710827

Lee, L. Y., & Sukco, B. M. (2010). The effects of cultural intelligence on expatriate performance: The moderating effects of international experience. *The International Journal of*

Human Resource Management, 21, 963–981.
http://dx.doi.org/10.1080/09585191003783397

Leedy, P. D., & Ormrod, J. E. (2010). *Practical research: Planning and design* (9th ed.). Upper
    Saddle River, NJ: Prentice Hall.

Leiba-O'Sullivan, S. (1999). The distinction between stable and dynamic cross-cultural
    competencies: implications for expatriate trainability. *Journal of International Business
    Studies, 30,* 709–725. http://dx.doi.org/10.1057/palgrave.jibs.8490835

Lincoln, Y. S., & Gupa, F. A. (1985). *Naturalistic inquiry.* Beverley Hills, CA: Sage.

Linehan, M., & Scullion, H. (2001). Repatriation of European female corporate executives: An
    empirical study. *International Journal of Human Resource Management, 13,* 254–267.
    http://dx.doi.org/10.1080/09585190110102369

Linehan, M., & Walsh, J. (2000). Work-family conflict and the senior female international
    manager. *British Journal of Management, 11,* 49–58. http://dx.doi.org/10.1111/1467-
    8551.11.s1.5

Littrell, L. N., Salas, E., Hess, K. P., Paley, M., & Riedel, S. (2006). Expatriate preparation: A
    critical analysis of 25 years of cross-cultural Research. *Human Resource Development
    Review, 5,* 355–388. http://dx.doi.org/10.1177/1534484306290106

Lundgren, L. (1998). The technical communicator's role in bridging the gap between Arab and
    American business environments. *Journal of Technical Writing and Communications,
    28,* 335–343. http://dx.doi.org/10.2190/U8AH-MQWD-F9L7-QAFA

Luthans, E., McCaul, H. S. & Dodd, N. G. (1985). Organizational commitment: A
    comparison of American Japanese and Korean Employees. *Academy of
    Management Journal, 28,* 213–219. http://dx.doi.org/10.2307/256069

Lynch, E. W. (1998). Conceptual framework: From culture shock to cultural learning. In E. Lynch
    & M. Hanson (Eds.), *Developing cross-cultural competence: A guide for working with
    children and their families* (3rd ed., pp. 20–40. Baltimore, MD: Brookes.

Mababaya, M. P. (2002). *The role of multinational companies in the Middle East: The case of
    Saudi Arabia.* London, England: Dissertation.com.

Macionis, J. J., & Plummer, K., (2008). *Sociology: A global introduction* (4th ed.). Harlow,
    England: Pearson Prentice Hall.

Maertz, C. P., Jr., Hassan, A., & Magnusson, P. (2009). When learning is not enough: A process
    model of expatriate adjustment as cultural cognitive dissonance reduction.
    Organizational Behavior and Human Decision Processes, 108, 66–78.
    http://dx.doi.org/10.1016/j.obhdp.2008.05.003

Malie, S., & Akir, O. (2012). Determinants for success in expatriation of Malaysian international
    corporations. *International Journal of Social, Behavioral, Educational, Economic, and
    Management Engineering, 6,* 140–143. Retrieved from waset.org/ Determinants-for-
    Success-in-Expatriation-of-Malaysian-International-Corporations[1].pdf

Mallehi, K. (2007). Effect of regulation on HRM: Private sector firms in Saudi Arabia.
    International Journal of Human Resource Management, 18, 85–88.
    http://dx.doi.org/10.1080/09585190601068359

Magnini, P., & Honeycutt, E. D. (2003) Learning orientation and the hotel expatriate manager
    experience. *Hospitality Management, 22,* 267–280. http://dx.doi.org/10:1016/so278-
    4319(03)00023-9.

Manpower. (2010). Talent Shortage Survey results. Retrieved from http://www.manpowergroup.com/wps/wcm/connect/130dc4b8-e53b-4c18-8baa-7ff108b4202b/Talent+Shortage+Survey+2010.pdf?MOD=AJPERES

Marshall, C., & Rossman, G. B. (2006). *Designing qualitative research* (4th ed.). London, England: Sage.

Marsick, V., & Watkins, K. (2001). Informal and incidental learning. In S. Merriam & R. Caffarella (Eds.), *Update on adult learning: New directions in adult and continuing education* (pp. 25–34). San Francisco, CA: Jossey-Bass.

Maslow A. H. (1954). *Motivation and personality.* New York, NY: Harper and Row.

Mayerhofer, H., Hartmann, L. C., & Herbert, A. (2004). Career management issues for flexpatriate international staff. *Thunderbird International Business Review, 46,* 647–666. http://dx.doi.org/10.1002/tie.20029

Mayerhofer, H., Hartmann, L. C., Michelitsch-Riedl, G. & Kollinger, I. (2004). Flexpatriate assignments: A neglected issue in global staffing. *International Journal of Human Resource Management, 15,* 1371–1389. http://dx.doi.org/10.1080/0958519042000257986

McCrae, R. R., & Costa, P. T. (1987). Validation of the five-factor model of personality across instruments and observers. *Journal of Personality and Social Psychology, 52,* 81–90. http://dx.doi.org/10.1016/S0191-8869(98)00016-6

McDonald, G. M. (1993). ET go home? The successful management of expatriate transfers. *Journal of Managerial Psychology, 8,* 18–29. http://dx.doi.org/10.1108/02683949310032758

Mencil, J. (2005). *Multi potentiality in the workplace: Person-environment fit, occupational outcomes, and emotional intelligence.* Unpublished manuscript.

Mendenhall, M. E., Dunbar, E., & Oddou, G. (1987). Expatriate selection, training and career-pathing: A review and critique. *Human Resource Management, 26,* 331–345. http://dx.doi.org/10.1002/hrm.3930260303

Mendenhall, M. E., & Oddou, G. (1985). The dimensions of expatriate acculturation. *Academy of Management Review, 10,* 39–47. Retrieved from http://aom.org/Publications/AMR/Academy-of-Management-Review.aspx

Meyer, J. P., & Allen, N. J. (1984) Testing the side bet theory of organizational commitment. *Journal of Applied Psychology, 6,* 372–378. http://dx.doi.org/10.1037//0021-9010.69.3.372

Mezias, J. M., & Scandura, T. A. (2005). A needs-driven approach to expatriate adjustment and career development: A multiple mentoring perspective. *Journal of International Business Studies, 36,* 519–538. http://dx.doi.org/10.1057/palgrave.jibs.8400159

Minkov, M., & Hofstede, G. (2011). The evolution of Hofstede's doctrine. *Cross Cultural Management: An International Journal, 18,* 10–20. http://dx.doi.org/10.1108/13527601111104269

Mol, S. T., Born, M. P., Willemsen, M. E., & van der Molen, H. T. (2005). Predicting expatriate job performance for selection purposes: A quantitative review. *Journal of Cross-Cultural Psychology, 36,* 590–620. http://dx.doi.org/10.1177/0022022105278544

Molinsky, A. L. (2007). Cross-cultural code-switching: The psychological challenges of adapting behavior in foreign cultural interactions. *Academy of Management Review, 32,* 622–640. http://dx.doi.org/10.2307/20159318

Moran, R. T., Harris, P. R., & Moran, S. V. (2007). *Managing cultural differences: Global leadership strategies for the 21st century* (7th ed.). Oxford, England: Butterworth-Heinemann.

Morgan, G. (1986). *Images of organization*. London, England: Sage.

Moustakas, C. E. (1994). *Phenomenological research methods*. Thousand Oaks, CA: Sage.

Mulholland, J. (1991). *The language of negotiation*. London, England: Routledge.

Naumann, E. (1993). Organizational predictors of expatriate job satisfaction. *Journal of International Business Studies, 10,* 61–80. http://dx.doi.org/10.1057/palgrave.jibs.8490225

Navas, M., Garcia, M. C., Sanchez, J., Rojas, A. J., Pumares, P., & Fernandez, J. S. (2005). Relative acculturation extended model (RAEM): New contributions with regard to the study of acculturation. *International Journal of Intercultural Relations, 29,* 21–37. http://dx.doi.org/10.1016/j.ijintrel.2005.04.001

Navas, M., Garcia, M. C., Sanchez, J., Rojas, A. J., Pumares, P., & Fernandez, J. S . (2007). Acculturation strategies and attitudes according to the relative acculturation extended model (RAEM): The perspectives of natives versus immigrants. *International Journal of Intercultural Relations, 31,* 67–86. http://dx.doi.org/10.1016/j.ijintrel.2006.08.002

Neill, J. (2008). *The expatriate venture: What role does cross-cultural training play and what theories guide research in the field?* Retrieved from www.uri.edu/research/Neill_Expatriate[1].pdf

Neuman, L. (2006). *Basics of social research: Qualitative and quantitative approaches.* London, England: Pearson/Allyn and Bacon

Newman, K. L., & Nollen, S. D. (1996). Culture and congruence: The fit between management practices and national culture. *Journal of International Business Studies, 27,* 753–779. http://dx.doi.org/10.1057/palgrave.jibs.8490152

Niblock, T., & Malik, M. (2007). *The political economy of Saudi Arabia*. New York, NY: Routledge.

Nicholson, N. (1984). A theory of work role transitions. *Administrative Science Quarterly, 29,* 172–191. http://dx.doi.org/10.2307/2393172

Nydell, M. K. (2012). *Understanding Arabs: A contemporary guide to Arab society* (5th ed.). London, England: Breasly.

Oberg, K. (1954, August). Culture shock. Presentation to the Women's Club of Rio De Janeiro, Brazil. Retrieved from http://citeseerx.ist.psu.edu/viewdoc/download?doi=10.1.1.461.5459&rep=rep1&type=pdf

Oberg, K. (1960). Culture shock: Adjustment to new cultural environments. *Practical Anthropologist, 7,* 177–182.

Olsson, M. (2009). The play's the thing: Theater professionals make sense of Shakespeare. *Library & Information Science Research, 32,* 272–280. http://dx.doi.org/10.1016/j.lisr.2010.07.009

Oshlyansky, L., Cairns, P., & Thimbleby, H. (2006). A cautionary tale: Hofstede's VSM revisited. *Proceedings of the 20th BCS HCI Group Conference, 2,* 11–15. Retrieved from www.cs.swansea.ac.uk/~csharold/cv/files/Oshlyansky_HCI06.pdf

Parker, P., & Inkson, K. (1999). New forms of career: The challenge to human resource management. *Asia Pacific Journal of Human Resources, 37*, 76–85. http://dx.doi.org/10.1177/103841119903700107

Patai, R. (2001). *The Arab mind.* Long Island, NY: Hatherleigh Press.

Patton, M. Q. (2002). *Qualitative research and evaluation methods* (3rd ed.). New York, NY: Sage.

Peiperl, M. A., & van der Sluis, E. C. (1999). *The experience of boundarylessness: Job change, extrinsic and intrinsic career success among early career MBAs.* Working Paper Series, No. 99-02, London Business School. Retrieved from www.opengrey.eu/handle/10068/564504

Peltokorpi, V., & Froese, F. J. (2009). Organizational expatriates and self-initiated expatriates: Who adjusts better to work and life in Japan? *International Journal of Human Resource Management, 20*, 1953–1957. http://dx.doi.org/10.1080/09585192.2012.725078

Peltokorpi, V., & Froese, F. J. (2011). The impact of expatriate personality traits on cross-cultural adjustment: A study with expatriates in Japan. *International Business Review. 21*, 734–746. http://dx.doi.org/10.1016/j.ibusrev.2011.08.006

Peng, M. D. (2009). *Global business* (2nd ed.). Cincinnatti, OH: South-Western Cengage Learning.

Perkins, S. J., & Hendry, C. (1999). Global compensation. In P. Joynt & B. Morton (Eds.), *The global HR manager* (pp. 115–143). London, England: Institute of Personnel and Development.

Peterson, M. (2009). *An introduction to decision theory.* Dubai, United Arab Emirates: Cambridge University Press.

Polanyi, M. (1958). *Personal knowledge: Towards a post-critical philosophy.* Chicago, IL: University of Chicago Press.

Polkinghorne, D. E. (2005). Language and meaning: Data collection in qualitative research. *Journal of Counseling Psychology, 52*, 137–145. http://dx.doi.org/10.1037/0022-0167.52.2.137

Pothukuchi, V., Damanpour, F., Choi, J., Chen, C. C., & Park, S. H. (2002). National and organizational culture differences and international joint venture performance. *Journal of International Business Studies, 33*, 243–265. Retrieved from http://papers.ssrn.com/sol3/papers.cfm?abstract_id=1005783##

Puck, J. F., Mohr, A. T., & Rygl, D. (2008). An empirical analysis of managers' adjustment to working in multi-national project teams in the pipeline and plant construction sector. *The International Journal of Human Resource Management, 19*, 2252–2267. http://dx.doi.org/10.1080/09585190802479488

Ratcliff, D. E. (2007). *Analytic induction as a qualitative research method of analysis.* Costa Mesa, CA: Vanguard University.

Rehman, A. (2008). *Dubai & co.: Global strategies for doing business in the Gulf States.* New York, NY: McGraw-Hill.

Rice, G. (2003). Islamic ethics and the implications for business. *Journal of Business Ethics. 18*, 345–358. http://dx.doi.org/10.1023/A:1005711414306

Richards, D. (1996). Strangers in a strange land: Expatriate paranoia and the dynamics of exclusion. *The International Journal of Human Resource Management, 7*, 553–571. http://dx.doi.org/10.1080/09585199600000143

Richardson, J. (2006). Self-directed expatriation: Family matters. *Personnel Review, 35*, 469–486. http://dx.doi.org/10.1108/00483480610670616

Richardson, J. (2009). *The independent expatriate: Academics abroad.* Saarbrücken, Germany: VDM Verlag.

Richardson, J., & Mallon, M. (2005). Career interrupted? The case of the self-directed expatriate. *Journal of World Business, 40*, 409–420. http://dx.doi.org/10.1016/j.jwb.2005.08.008

Richardson, J., & McKenna, S. (2002). Leaving and experiencing: Why academics expatriate and how they experience expatriation. *Career Development International, 7*, 67–78. http://dx.doi.org/10.1108/13620430210421614

Richardson, J., & McKenna, S. (2003). International experience and academic careers: What do academics have to say? *Personnel. Review, 32*, 774–795.

Ritchie, J., Lewis, J., & Elam, G. (2003). Designing and selecting samples. In J. Ritchie & J. Lewis (Eds.), *Qualitative research practice. A guide for social science students and researchers* (pp.77–108) Thousand Oaks, CA: Sage

Rose, R. C., & Kumar, S. (2008). A review on individual differences and cultural intelligence. *The Journal of International Social Research, 1*, 504–522. Retrieved from www.sosyalarastirmalar.com/cilt1/sayi4/sayi4pdf/rose.pdf

Rose, R. C., Ramalu, S., Uli, J., & Kumar, N. (2010). Expatriate performance in overseas assignments: The role of Big Five personality. *Asian Social Science, 6*, 104–113. http://dx.doi.org/10.5539/ass.v6n9p104

Rousseau, D. M. (1989). Psychological and implied contracts in organizations. *Employee Responsibilities and Rights Journal, 2*, 121–139. http://dx.doi.org/101007/BF01384942

Rousseau, D. M. (2001). Schema, promise and mutuality: The building blocks of the psychological contracts. *Journal of Occupational and Organizational Psychology, 74*, 511–541. http://dx.doi.org/10.1348/096317901167505

Sakala, C., Gyte, G., Henderson, S., Neilsen, J. P., & Horey, D. (2001). Consumer-professional partnership to improve research: The experience of Cochrane Collaborations Pregnancy and Childbirth Group. *Birth, 28*, 133–137. http://dx.doi.org/10.1046/j.1523-536X.2001.00133.x

Salkind, N. J. (2008). *Exploring research* (7th ed.). London, England: Prentice Hall.

Schein, E. H. (1985). *How culture forms, develops and changes.* San Francisco, CA: Jossey Bass.

Schein, E. H. (1995, June). *Organizational culture as a facilitator or inhibitor of organizational transformation.* Working paper presented to the Inaugural Assembly of Chief Executives and Employers, Singapore. Retrieved from *www*.dspace.mit.edu/1/swp-383133296477[1].pdf

Schein, E. H. (2004). *Organizational culture and leadership* (3rd ed.). San Francisco, CA: Jossey-Bass.

251

Schmidt, F. L., & Hunter, J. E. (1992). Development of a causal model of processes Determining job performance. *Current Directions in Psychological Science, 1*, 89–92. http://dx.doi.org/10.1111/1467-8721.ep10768758

Schneider, S. C., & Asakawa, K. (1995). American and Japanese expatriate adjustment: A psychoanalytic perspective. *Human Relations, 48*, 1109–1127. http://dx.doi.org/10.1177/001872679504801001

Schuler, R. S., & Tarique, I. (2007). International human resource management: A thematic update and suggestions for future research. *International Journal of Human Resource Management, 18*, 714–744. http://dx.doi.org/10.1080/09585190701246590

Scurry, T., Rodriguez, J. K., & Bailouni, S. (2013). Narratives of identity of self-initiated expatriates in Qatar. *Career Development International, 18*, 12–33. http://dx.doi.org/10.1108/13620431311305926

Searle, W., & Ward, C. (1990). The prediction of psychological and social cultural adjustment during cross cultural transitions. *International Journal of Intercultural Relations, 14*, 449–464. http://dx.doi.org/10.1016/0147-1767(90)90030-Z

Selmer, J. (2001). Psychological barriers to adjustment and how they affect coping strategies: Western business expatriates in China. *International Journal of Human Resource Management, 12*, 151–165. http://dx.doi.org/10.1080/09585190122767

Selmer, J., & Lauring, J. (2010). Self-initiated academic expatriates: Inherent demographics and reasons to expatriate. *European Management Review, 7*, 19–29. http://dx.doi.org/10.1057/emr.2010.15

Selmer, J., & Leung, A. S. M. (2003). Provision and adequacy of corporate support to male expatriate spouses. *Personnel Review, 32*, 9–21. http://dx.doi.org/10.1108/00483480310454691

Shaffer, M. A., & Harrison, D. A. (1998). Expatriates' psychological withdrawal from international assignments: Work, non-work, and family influences. *Personnel Psychology, 51*, 87–118. http://dx.doi.org/10.1111/j.1744-6570.1998.tb00717.x

Shaffer, M. A., Harrison, D. A., Gregersen, H., Black, J. S., & Ferzandi, L. A. (2006). You can take it with you: Individual differences and expatriate effectiveness. *Journal of Applied Psychology, 91*, 109–125. http://dx.doi.org/10.1037/0021-9010.91.1.109

Shin, S. J., Morgeson, F. P., & Campion, M. A. (2003). *Expatriate assignments: Understanding the skill, ability, personality, and behavioral requirements of working abroad.* Purdue CIBER Working Papers, Paper 20. Retrieved from http://docs.lib.purdue.edu/ciberwp/20

Siders, M. A., George, G., & Dharwadkar, R. (2001). The relationship of internal and external commitment foci to objective performance measures. *Academy of Management Journal, 44*, 570–579. http://dx.doi.org/10.2307/3069371

Simon, M. (2006). *Dissertation and scholarly research: Recipes for success.* Dubuque, IA: Kendall Hunt.

Sinangil, H. K., & Ones, D. S. (2001). Expatriate management. In N. Anderson, D. S. Ones, H. K. Sinangil & C. Viswesvaran (Eds.), *Handbook of industrial, work & organizational psychology* (pp. 424–443). London, England: Sage.

Smith, C.R. (1994). *The career consequences of dual-career status: Implications for Organizational career development* (Unpublished doctoral thesis, University of Western Australia, Perth, Australia. Retrieved from www.pijmt.com/1/career_consequences_of_dualcareer_status_Implications_for_Organizational_career_development[1].pdf

Smith, J. A. (2004). Reflecting on the development of interpretative phenomenological analysis and its contribution to qualitative research in psychology. *Qualitative Research in Psychology, 1*, 39–54. http://dx.doi.org/10.1191/1478088704qp004oa

Smith, J. A. (2007). Hermeneutics, human sciences and health: Linking theory and practice. *International Journal of Qualitative Studies on Health and Well-Being, 2*, 3–11. http://dx.doi.org/10.1080/17482620601016120

Smith, J. A., Flowers, P., & Larkin, M. (2009). *Interpretive phenomenological research: Theory, method and research.* London, England: Sage.

Smith, J. A., Flowers, P. & Osborn, M. (1997). Interpretative phenomenological analysis and health psychology. In L. Yardley (Ed.), *Material discourses and health* (pp. 68–91). London, England: Routledge.

Smith, J. A., Jarman, M. & Osborn, M. (1999). Doing interpretative phenomenological Analysis, In M. Murray & K. Chamberlain (eds.), *Qualitative health psychology: theories & methods* (pp. 218-240). London, England: Sage.

Smith, M. P. (2005). Transnational urbanism revisited. *Journal of Ethnic and Migration Studies, 31*, 235–244. http://dx.doi.org/10.1080/1369183042000339909

Snape, D., & Spencer, L. (2003). The foundations of qualitative research. In J. Ritchie & J. Lewis, (Eds.), *Qualitative research practice: A guide for social science students and researchers* (pp. 2–10). London, England: Sage.

Solomon, C. M. (1994). Success abroad depends on more than job skills. *Personnel Journal, 4*, 51–59. Retrieved from http://www.workforce.com/articles/success-abroad-depends-on-more-than-job-skills

Sparrow P. R. (1999). International rewards systems: To converge or not to converge? In C. Brewster & H. Harris (Eds.), *International HRM–Contemporary issues in Europe* (pp. 103–119். London, England: Routledge.

Stenning, B. W. (1994). Expatriate management: Lessons from the British in India. *The International Journal of Human Resource Management, 5*, 385–404. http://dx.doi.org/10.1080/09585199400000023

Stierle, C., van Dick, R., & Wagner, U. (2002). Success or failure? Personality, family, and intercultural orientation as determinants of expatriate managers' success. *Zeitschrift fur Socialpsychologie, 33*, 209–218. http://dx.doi.org/10.1024//0044-3514.33.4.209

Suutari, V., & Brewster, C. (1998, June). *Expatriate management practices and expatriates' preferences toward such practices: A survey among Finnish expatriates.* Conference proceedings of the 6th conference on IHRM, Paderborn, Germany [CD].

Suutari, V., & Brewster, C. (2000). Making their own way: International experience through self-initiated foreign assignments. *Journal of World Business, 35*, 417–436. http://dx.doi.org/10.1016/S1090-9516(00)00046-8

Suzuki, N. (1998). Inside *NGOs: Learning to manage conflicts between headquarters and field offices.* London, England: Intermediate Technologies.

Swagler, M. A., & Jome, L. M. (2005). The effects of personality and acculturation on the adjustment of North American sojourners in Taiwan. *Journal of Counseling Psychology, 42*, 527–536. http://dx.doi.org/10.1037/0022-0167.52.4.527

Swales, S. (2000). Goals, creativity and achievement: Commitment in contemporary organizations. *Creativity and Innovative Management, 9*, 185–195. http://dx.doi.org/10.1111/1467-8691.00171

Takeuchi, R., Yun, S., & Russell, J. E. A. (2002). Antecedents and consequences of the perceived adjustment of Japanese expatriates in the USA. *International Journal of Human Resource Management, 13*, 1224–1244. doi:10.1080/09585190210149493

Takeuchi, R., Yun, S., & Tesluk, P. (2002). An examination of cross-over and spillover effects of spousal and expatriate cross-cultural adjustment on expatriate outcomes. *Journal of Applied Psychology, 87*, 655–666. http://dx.doi.org/10.1037//0021-9010.87.4.655

Tams, S., & Arthur, M. B. (2007). Studying careers across cultures: Distinguishing international, cross-cultural, and globalization perspectives. *Career Development International, 12*, 86–98. http://dx.doi.org/10.1108/13620430710724848

Tayeb, M. (1988). *Organizations and national culture: A comparative Analysis.* London, England: Sage.

Tayeb, M. (1994). Organizations and national culture: Methodology considered. *Organization Studies, 15*, 429–446. http://dx.doi.org/10.1177/017084069401500306

Tayeb, M. (2005). *International human resource management.* New York, NY: Oxford University Press.

Tharenou, P., & Caulfield, N. (2010). Will I stay or will I go? Explaining repatriation by self-initiated expatriates. *Academy of Management Journal, 53*, 1009–1028. http://dx.doi.org/10.5465/AMJ.2010.54533183

Thomas, D. C., & Osland, J. S. (2004). Mindful communication. In J. S. Osland, M. E. Turner, D. A. Kolb, & I. W. Rubin (Eds.), *The organizational behavior reader* (8th ed., pp. 295–306). Upper Saddle River, NJ: Pearson Prentice Hall.

Thorn, K. (2009). The relative importance of motives for international self-initiated mobility.

Career Development International, 14, 441–464. http://dx.doi.org/10 1108/13620430910989843

Thorn, K. J. (2008). *Flight of the kiwi: An exploration of motives and behaviours of self-initiated mobility* (Doctoral thesis, Massey University, Auckland, New Zealand). Retrieved from http://hdl.handle.net/10179/834

Triandis, H. C. (1984). A theoretical framework for the more efficient construction of culture assimilators. *International Journal of Intercultural Relations, 8*, 301–330. http://dx.doi.org/10.1016/0147-1767(84)90029-4

Triandis, H. C. (1988). Collectivism and individualism: A reconceptualization of a basic concept in cross-cultural psychology. In G. K. Verma & C. Bagley (Eds.), *Personality, attitudes, and cognitions* (pp. 60–95). London, England: MacMillan.

Triandis, H. C. (1989). The self and social behavior in differing cultural contexts. *Psychological Review, 96*, 506–520. http://dx.doi.org/10.1037/0033-295X.96.3.506

Triandis, H. C. (1990). Cross-cultural studies of individualism and collectivism. In J. Berman (Ed.), *Nebraska Symposium on Motivation, 1989* (pp. 41–133). Lincoln: University of Nebraska Press.

Triandis, H. C. (1995). *Individualism & collectivism.* Boulder, CO: Westview Press.

Triandis, H. C. (2004). The many dimensions of culture. *Academy of Management Executives, 18*, 88–93. http://dx.doi.org/10.5465/AME.2004.12689599

Triandis, H. C., Brislin, R. W., & Hui, C. H. (1988). Cross-cultural training across the individualism and collectivism divide. *International Journal of Intercultural Relations, 12,* 269–289. http://dx.doi.org/10.1016/0147-1767(88)90019-3

Triandis, H. C., Malpass, R. S. & Davidson, F. (1973). Psychology and culture. *Annual Review of Psychology, 24,* 355–378. http://dx.doi.org/10.1146/annurev.ps.24.020173.002035

Triandis, H. C., & Suh. E. M. (2002). Cultural influences on personality. *Annual Review of Psychology, 53,* 133–160. http://dx.doi.org/10.1146/annurev.psych.53.100901.135200

Trochim, W. M. (2006). *The research methods knowledge base* (2nd ed.). Cincinnati, OH: Atomic Dog.

Trompenaars, F. (1993). *Riding the waves of culture.* London, England: Brearly.

Trompenaars, F., & Hampden-Turner, C. (2000). *Riding the waves of culture: Understanding diversity in global business* (2nd ed.). New York, NY: McGraw Hill.

Trumbull, E., Rothstein-Fisch, C., Greenfield, P. M., & Quiroz, B. (2001). *Bridging cultures between home and school: A guide for teachers.* Mahwah, NJ: Erlbaum.

Tsui, A. S., Nifadkar, S. S., & Ou, A. Y. (2007). Cross-national, cross-cultural organizational behavior research: Advances, gaps, and recommendations. *Journal of Management, 33,* 426–478. http://dx.doi.org/10.1177/0149206307300818

Tung, R. L. (1981). Selection and training of personnel for overseas assignments. *Colombia Journal of World Business, 16,* 68–78. http://dx.doi.org/10.1108/PR-11-2013-0216

Tung, R. L. (1982). Selecting and training procedures of U. S., European, and Japanese multinational corporations, *California Management Review, 25,* 57–71. http://dx.doi.org/10.2307/41164993

Tung, R. L. (1987). Expatriate assignments: Enhancing success and minimizing failure. *Academy of Management Executive, 1,* 117–126. http://dx.doi.org/10.5465/AME.1987.4275826

Tung, R. L. (1988). *The new expatriates: Managing human resources abroad.* Cambridge, MA: Ballinger.

Tung, R. L. (2004). Female expatriates: The model global manager? *Organizational Dynamics, 33,* 243–253. Retrieved from http://www.cipd.co.uk/search/results/bookrow.asp?ID=194068

Tziner, A., & Birati, A. (1996). Assessing employee turnover costs: A revised approach. *Human Resource Management Review, 6,* 113–121. http://dx.doi.org/10.1016/S1053-4822(96)90015-7

Van der Zee, K. I., & Van Oudenhoven, J. P. (2001). The Multicultural Personality Questionnaire: Reliability and validity of self and other ratings of multicultural effectiveness. *Journal of Research in Personality, 35,* 278–288. http://dx.doi.org/10.1006/jrpe.2001.2320

Van Manen, M. (1990). *Researching lived experience: Human science for an action sensitive pedagogy.* London, Ontario: Althouse Press.

Van Vianen, A. E. M., De Pater, I. E., Kristof-Brown, A. L., & Johnson, E. C. (2004). Dimensions of cultural experiences affecting expatriates' cross-cultural adjustment: Cultural similarity and values fit. *Academy of Management Journal, 47,* 697–709. Retrieved from http://bizfaculty.nus.edu/publications/3507

Vance, C. (2005). The personal quest for building global competence: A taxonomy of self-initiating career path strategies for gaining business experience abroad. *Journal of World Business, 40,* 374–385. http://dx.doi.org/10.1016/j.jwb.2005.08.005

Varner, I. (2002). Successful expatriation and organization strategies. *Review of Business, 23*, 8–12. Retrieved from http://www.freepatentsonline.com/article/Review-Business/87211787.html

Vince, R., Sutcliffe, K., & Olivera, F. (2002). Organizational learning: New directions. *British Journal of Management, 13*, S1–S6. http://dx.doi.org/10.1111/1467-8551.13.s2.1

Walker, W. (2007). Ethical considerations in phenomenological research. *Nursing Research, 19*, 309–314. http://dx.doi.org/10.7748/nr2007.04.14.3.36.c6031

Walker, F., Walker, Y., & Schmitz, J. (2003). *Doing business internationally.* New York, NY: McGraw-Hill.

Wang, L., Bishop, J. W., Chen, X. & Scott, K. D. (2002). Collectivist orientation as a predictor of affective organizational commitment: A study conducted in China. *International Journal of Organizational Analysis, 10*, 226–239. http://dx.doi.org/10.1108/eb028951

Ward, C., Bochner, S., & Furnham, A. (2001). *The psychology of culture shock* (2nd ed.). Philadelphia, PA: Routledge.

Ward, C., & Kennedy, A. (1992). Locus of control, mood disturbance and social difficulty during cross-cultural transitions. *International Journal of Intercultural Relations, 16*, 175–194. http://dx.doi.org/10.1016/0147-1767(92)90017-O

Weick, K. E., & Sutcliffe, K. M. (2005). Organizing and the process of sensemaking. *Organization Science, 16*, 409–421. http://dx.doi.org/10.1287/orsc.1050.0133

Wertz, F. (2005). Phenomenological research methods for counseling psychology. *Journal of Counseling Psychology, 52*, 167–177. http://dx.doi.org/10.1037/0022-0167.52.2.167

Williams, J. (2010). *Don't they know it's Friday? A cross-cultural guide for business and life in the Gulf.* Dubai, United Arab Emirates: Gulf Business Books/Motivate Publishing.

Willis, J. (2007). *Foundations of qualitative research: Interpretive and critical approaches.* Thousand Oaks, CA: Sage.

Woods, P. (2003). Performance management of Australian and Singaporean expatriates. *International Journal of Manpower, 24*, 517–534. http://dx.doi.org/10.1108/01437720310491062

Yan, A., Zhu, G. & Douglas, T. H. (2002). International assignments for career building: A model of agency relationships and psychological contracts. *Academy of Management Review, 27*, 373–391. Retrieved from http://aom.org/Publications/AMR/Academy-of-Management-Review.aspx

Yavas, U., & Yasin, M. M. (1999). Organizational significance and application of computer skills: A culturally-based empirical examination. *Cross Cultural Management, 6*, 11–21. http://dx.doi.org/10.1108/13527609910796997

Yeo, S., Ling, P., Mazzolini, M., Giridharan, B., Goerke, V., & Hall, D. (2011, June 29–July 1). *Demonstrating quality.* Paper presented at the Australian Universities Forum, Melbourne, Australia. Retrieved from http://www.academia.edu/2847770/Ensuring_quality_in_undergraduate_curriculum_reform_Experience_in_Hong_Kong

Yin, R. K. (2003). *Case study research: Design and methods* (3rd ed.). Thousand Oaks, CA: Sage.

Zelina, M. (1996). *Stratégie a metódy rozvoja osobnosti dieťaťa.* Bratislava: IRIS.

Zhang, Y., & Wildemuth, B. (2009). Thematic content analysis. In B. Wildemuth (Ed.),
Applications of social research methods to questions in information and library science
(pp. 308–319). Westport, CT: Libraries Unlimited.

APPENDIX A

PARTICIPANT SOLICITATION LETTER

Research Focus
This research examines how adults who have independently relocated to a foreign country for employment adjustment to their expatriate experience and how they make-sense of the experiences during this period.

Why is This Research Needed?
There is a great deal of academic literature emphasizing the negative consequences of the inability to adjust. International psychology and sociology scholars suggest that expatriation can disturb people's sense of identity, result in psychological illness and create a lack of lasting social connections. For this reason, it is important to understand how people who self-initiate expatriation learn to positively adjust, grow and prosper as a result of changes in their physical and social environments.

Who Can Participate? You qualify to participate in this research if you:
• have personally initiated a move to a foreign country for employment reasons all your own;
• have lived and worked successfully in the education field as an expatriate for at least two years;
• are fluent in the English language.

What is involved?
The research process involves participating in a 60 to 90 minute face-to-face interview about the story of your life and living abroad, specifically areas of adjustment as you remember them and how you made sense of them.

The interview does not include everything that has ever happened to you as an expatriate. Instead, I will ask you to focus on a few key things in your experience—a few key events, characters, and ideas having to do with your life in a foreign country and your decision to remain there. I will ask you about high points, low points and challenges you have faced. Finally, I will ask you to reflect on what you have learned from your experiences of living in a new physical and social environment.

There is no right or wrong answers to my questions, simply to tell me about some of the most important things that have happened in your life and how you have processed and made sense of them. Please know that my purpose in doing this interview is not to figure out what is wrong with you or to do some kind of deep clinical analysis! The interview is for research purposes only, and its main goal is simply to hear your story and to understand your experience of adjustment to your new situation.

Everything you say is voluntary, anonymous, and confidential. The interview will be electronically recorded and will be transcribed into a document form. I will send you the transcript by email and will ask you to review it for accuracy. At this time (if you choose) you can make any revisions or corrections that you feel may more accurately reflect what you meant at the time of the interview. You will also be asked to sign a participant consent form. This form is a legal and ethical requirement for participation in human research.

Benefits to you
The interview is designed to be a positive and energizing experience for you. By telling your story, you will gain personal insight and greater self-awareness through reflecting on your own experience. Your interview will be contributing to academic research guiding the theoretical and practical understanding of environmental psychology.

I will provide a safe emotional environment for the interview. The potential for risk is highly unlikely. If, however, you find that you are experiencing difficult emotions during in the course of the interview, you have the right to stop at any time. You may also choose to skip any questions.

Participant Confidentiality
Your identity and confidentiality will be safeguarded. All identifying information (such as names, addresses, etc.) will be removed when the audio recordings are transcribed. No personal information associated with identity will be released to any other party without written permission. Any quotes used in the final report will remain anonymous.

About the Researcher
This research is to fulfill the doctoral level requirements in Psychology at the University of the Rockies in Colorado Springs, Colorado, USA. I currently hold a Master's degree in Adult Education and have qualified as a doctoral candidate. I currently live in the UAE and have first-hand experience with many of the physical, social, and psychological challenges associated with self-initiated expatriation as I myself am a self-initiated expatriate. I have been in Education for 27 years as a teacher and administrator. I believe that research into the physical, social, and psychological aspects of self-initiated expatriation can provide significant insights into human-environment relationships, including what creates and sustains a sense of belonging, and how people learn to thrive in new places.

Contact Information
To participate in this research, contact David Nelson to arrange an interview time.
Email:
Skype:

APPENDIX B: INTERVIEW GUIDE
INTERVIEW GUIDE

The main issues to be questioned and explored are listed below. It is the intention that all topics be addressed with each participant but the order and flow may vary with each participant.

Introduction
Each interview will begin with an introduction of the researcher, the topic and the purpose of the interview. The guidelines and confidentiality will be reviewed and the informed consent form signed. Participant demographics will also be reviewed at this point.

Hello and thank you for your participation. I am Dave Nelson, a Doctoral student enrolled in the University of the Rockies. I am also a Self- Initiated Expatriate, which is why I find myself interested and involved in this research. Let's talk about this project. This research project is concerned with the process of adjustment. I am particularly interested in your personal experiences in adjusting to your new life situation as a Self-Initiated Expatriate. I am going to ask you about what issues and problems you encountered during the transition from your home culture to the current culture you are now a part of. I would like to know your feelings regarding the differences and similarities, what you found to be an easy area of transition and what areas you found to be difficult. I am also eager to hear what you believe was the most difficult component of adjusting as well as what helped you adjust and if you have any thoughts regarding what support or resources could have helped make your adjustment easier.

Some details regarding the interview. There is no right or wrong answers. Your thoughts and opinions, the feelings associated with those experiences is what I am asking you to share. You have complete freedom to choose what details and information you provide to me. If at any time a question makes you uncomfortable or you do not wish to answer please let me know and we will move on to another topic. If you have any questions during the interview, feel free to ask me.

The interview will last approximately sixty to ninety minutes. The interview is being recorded to allow for accurate transcription. I may also take some notes during the interview. All information will be confidential. I will make available to you copies of all recordings, transcripts and notes concerning your interview if you would like them.

Consent form. In order for you to participate, I need you to sign an informed consent form. Please be aware that you may withdraw this consent at any point in the research process. The highlights of the consent form are to ensure your anonymity and confidentiality. Your records will be stored for five years in a secure environment then destroyed or returned to you if possible. Demographics. Next, I need to collect some general information regarding your background. If we could answer the following items (use participant DATA Form)

Now that we have all the technical needs done the main part of the interview aims to get information about the participants' process of adjustment. I will ask questions about your life about how adjusted you feel and what you believe attributed to that feeling and if you feel that any of those feelings can or may change. With these questions I will also ask you to reflect on the process of adjusting to your new environment. How satisfied you feel and what you consider to have been easy and what you think are the more difficult aspects of the process and your current situation.
Questions

Socio-cultural *overall comfort level in relation to new environment*

    Work *comfort level in reference to the new job responsibilities and the new work environment.*

> Before coming here, did you receive any multicultural education to help you to adjust to your new environment? How about your family/spouse? Did they receive any training?
>
> Describe what your experiences are regarding your workplace (or school) and what it is like for you to meet people of different cultures? How confident are you in performing work activities? Working with your co-workers? How satisfied are you with the daily routines? Are there things you don't understand? Why do you think you feel this way?
>
> *Follow up*
> *How do you expect to be treated as an expatriate professional?*

General *comfort level towards the general living conditions and cultural practices of the new host culture:*

Initial experiences upon arriving in the region? What support did you have upon your arrival? (For example, organizational, friends, church support) How did this impact your initial experiences?

Describe your experiences in adapting to the new cultural groups of this region, their laws and customs. Are there aspects of the new national culture you find particularly easy/difficult to adjust to? What do you like about living in the region? And/or dislike about living here? (Explore feelings of anger, depression or positive feelings and what causes these feelings).

Follow ups?
How do you cope/deal with this? How have your family members/significant others adapted to their new and different living conditions here? How do you/they manage the difficulties or challenges of living here?

Interaction *comfort level in communicating and interacting with members of the host culture.*

> How confident are you in performing social activities or tasks? Where have you made new friends? (Explore what is important to the person, for example, expat clubs, social networks, church and so forth).
>
> *Follow up*
> *Describe how new friendships may have assisted you in adjusting to the life in*
> *The region. What are your views of social support with regards to adapting to your life here?*
>
> How would you describe your contact with nationals? What is your experience with interpersonal relationships in nationals? How satisfied are you with social relations in your new environment?

In your opinion, what are the most important factors that assisted you to adjust to living in a new country? What factors do you think hinder the adjustment process?

Is there anything else you would like to tell me? (The objective here is to find out if there are some aspects the participants think I have left out or they wish to add something to things they have said earlier.)

Concluding remarks.

Thank you for participating in the interview. I hope it was a pleasant experience I would greatly appreciate any feedback about the experience of the interview. May I contact you again if I need to follow up or clarify anything?

APPENDIX C

INFORMED CONSENT FORM

Informed Consent Form for a Phenomenological Study Regarding the Perceptions and Experiences of Self-Initiated Expatriates

You are being invited to participate in a research project conducted by David Dushan Nelson, who is a doctoral student at University of the Rockies. You are invited to participate in a research study about feelings and meaning attached to life experiences of Self-Initiated Expatriates working in the Gulf Coast Council region.

You will be asked to participate in an interview process in which you will respond to questions concerning your experiences and the feelings you experienced and any meaning you have attached to the experience, that will take about 1-2 hours of your time (there may be the need for follow up discussion which should be no more than an additional hour total.
The potential risks associated with this study include a possibility of the resurfacing and dealing with emotionally unpleasant or traumatic experiences. This study aims to explore how these self -initiated expatriates perceived and experienced issues and adjustment, if and how adjustment to the living conditions of this region were accomplished, and if there are any factors that have not yet been discussed or identified. This study seeks to examine a number of crucial questions, the answers to which may present invaluable information to the organizations which seek recruitment of these self-initiated expatriates and also to the self-initiated expatriates themselves.

If you have decided to participate in this project, please understand that your participation is voluntary and that you have the right to withdraw your consent or discontinue participation at any time with no penalty. You may withdraw verbally at any time before, during, or after the interview, via telephone communication or through email communication. Upon withdrawal, an official confirmation email will be sent from the researcher to the participant stating that all paper information will be shredded, audio-recordings from in-depth interviews, and the electronic transcription of the interview are destroyed. You also have the right to refuse to answer any question(s) for any reason with no penalty.

In addition, your individual privacy will be maintained in all publications or presentations resulting from this study. To ensure confidentiality, the researcher will code each interview transcript and subsequent study field notes to preserve the privacy of the participants. The code will consist of an alphanumeric system comprised of the first and last letter of the participants surname followed by a three digit number. The assigned code will serve to identify each participant in the study. The list of participants' names and numbers will remain in a sealed envelope in a safety deposit box separate from the list of participant numbers and study data. All audio and video recorded interviews will be maintained in a safe deposit box for a period of five years from the publication of the research. Confidentiality protocols will remain in effect during this period. At the end of the five year period, all audio and video recordings will be destroyed. All participants are entitled to receive a copy of any audio or video recordings in which they appear.

If you have any questions regarding this project, you may contact the researcher at ███████████████████ or at ████████ If you have questions regarding your rights as a research participant or any concerns regarding this project, you may contact my advisor, Dr. Irene F. Stein, at University of the Rockies, or you may report concerns – confidentially, if you wish – to the UoR Chairperson of the Institutional Review Board at ire@rockies.edu.

A copy of this consent form will be provided to you.

I understand the above information and voluntarily consent to participate in the research. I further attest that I am at least 18 years of age.

Signature of Participant: _____ Date: _____

IRB Approval Number: _____ IRB Expiration Date:

For questions regarding the research, Dr. Nelson may be contacted at david@credereconsultingservices.com.

Credere Consulting Services
Life & Executive Coaching, Motivational Speaking, Leadership Development